THE
PRIVATE PRACTICE
FIELD GUIDE

Daniel A. Franz

"I HAVE AN *IDEA*. WHO WANTS TO COME ALONG WITH ME?"

- SETH GODIN, TRIBES

THE
PRIVATE PRACTICE
FIELD GUIDE

For my wife Michelle, and my daughters Emalie and Elaina;
it's because of you I do what I do.

© Daniel A. Franz 2011
Book layout and cover design: Nicole L. Diana

TABLE OF CONTENTS

CHAPTER ONE
QUESTIONS AND ANSWERS, 7

CHAPTER TWO
MY STORY, 15

CHAPTER THREE
THE BUSINESS OF BUILDING A PRIVATE PRACTICE, 25

CHAPTER FOUR
MARKETING YOUR PRACTICE, 63

CHAPTER FIVE
YOUR WEBSITE AS YOUR PRIMARY MARKETING STRATEGY, 89

CHAPTER SIX
YOU ARE THE BUSINESS- THE PERSONAL SIDE OF PRIVATE PRCTICE, 107

ACKNOWLEDGEMENTS, 116
APPENDIX, 118

1

Questions & Answers

Why I am writing this and Why I think you should be in private practice

I truly believe that having more therapists, social workers, counselors, and psychologists working in their own self-directed, successful, and authentic private practices will allow us, the helping professional community, to help more people, in a more positive and effective manner.

More people receiving better quality mental health care, emotional support, and healing will improve the quality of the communities in which we live. By improving the communities we live in, we slowly help improve the quality of the world. Not only are we able to improve the quality of life for more people, but we are also able to further improve the quality of life for ourselves and our profession. We further legitimize our field, share it's true value, and can better describe it's value to others.

That's a fairly big and bold opening statement. But one I firmly believe in. It's an idea I have thought about, pondered, and shaped over the past several years. Let's break it down a bit.

Who this book is for

I think we all know who we are – the helping professionals community. Those people who went through college and then on to a master's program and maybe even a Ph.D. to study their passion for helping people under an accredited curriculum with a name like: licensed mental health counselor, social worker, marriage and family therapist, psychologist, clinical psychologist, etc. You probably even have a license or several licenses with a variety of initials, or at least you are working towards one. You may even have a whole set of other initials after your name specifying a variety of areas of study or specializations you have taken the time to work through on your own after graduation.

What you don't have to start your business is an MBA, or at least I know I didn't have one when I got started. Nor did I have a lick of business sense. I got lucky – very lucky – with some of the encounters I had that lead me in to private practice. I spent was fortunate to spend a considerable amount of time in the business and marketing of several clinical operations and a few non-clinical businesses.

> "The goal here is to provide you with all the nuts and bolts, all the details, all the behaviors, attitudes, and ideas you need, free of fluff and filler."

On the other hand, I made a ton of mistakes, too. In fact you could say I made more than $1,000,000 worth of mistakes before I got here. I'll tell you more about that in a later section. I'm writing this so you don't have to do that. I would hope that with this guide, and a little bit of hard work and maybe some coaching if you need it, you can be in your own successful and authentic private practice fairly quickly – and with far less expense, far fewer mistakes, and a lot less frustration.

This book is for those of you in the helping field ready to start a private practice, or improve the one you already operate.

Why a "Field Manual"?

If you've ever read or reviewed any kind of field manual, trail guide, hiking guide, or state park map, you know that they are the bare bones, nuts and bolts fact whether you like them or not. No fluff, no "rah rah"; just plain, to-the-point "This is what to do". That's what the goal is here. I want you to have

GUIDED INSPIRATION

One of the best trail guides I've ever read is the North Carolina – Georgia Guide to the Appalachian Trail. It lays out several hundred miles of path bit-by-bit. Where to stop, where to get water, best places to set up camp, worst places to set up camp, etc. It is brutally honest – as I intend to be here. The best bit of honesty in that guide was its description in handling bears along the trail:

Bears that have lost their fear of humans may "bluff charge" to get you to drop your food or backpack. If you encounter a black bear, it will probably run away. If it does not (you mean there is an option?!), back away slowly, watching the bear but not making direct eye-contact. Do not run away or play dead. If a bear attacks, fight for all you are worth.

Is starting a private practice a life-or-death situation on some backwoods trail? No. But it might mean the survival of your true and authentic self. It might be your best chance at self-fulfillment. The path to a successful and authentic private practice is full of difficulties and revelations. There are plenty of "bears" along the way. There are plenty of obstacles to prevent you from getting to where you want to be. When you encounter one, this is the time to "fight for all you are worth," you will find the end result is well worth fighting for. This field manual is intended to make the trip easier and push you towards achieving success.

The goal here is to provide you with all the nuts and bolts, all the details, all the behaviors, attitudes, and ideas you need, free of fluff and filler. I'm going to share all the ups and downs, good and bad, scenic vistas and rotten climbs that I am aware of. It might not always be the most pleasant information, it might conflict with what you thought or what you are doing now, but it is the honest-to-goodness path that I have used to build my successful and authentic private practice, and how I have helped others build theirs. I encourage you to push forward and try the things that scare you – if you need help, there is an entire community out here to help you. I want to help as well. Feel free to email me.

What does "self-directed, successful, and authentic" mean?
Aren't those some great buzzwords? I started using them because I really meant them; I really felt them.

Then I realized a lot of other people liked them too… Apparently these are great "marketing buzzwords." They may be interpreted as a bit disingenuous. But I'm not willing to compromise on them, or give them up, so I will have to define them in the specific sense I mean.

Self-directed
It is a simple as "directing yourself" – you get to make the choices that impact your professional and personal life. This may be a scary proposition. It's possible you have become so used to that agency you work for making those decisions for you: when to show up, what times to work, when to go home, when to take a vacation, how much vacation to take, what clients you are going to see, when you are going to see them, how much to earn, when you will be paid, when you will use the restroom… All decisions that you have some small amount of input in when working for another entity, but mostly leave to human resources departments or "The Boss."

In private practice, those decisions are all yours. You get to make good and bad decisions about all those things I just listed and more.

Want to take a week off, take it whenever you want. Want to take a month off? It's yours.
Of course, just like any area in your life where we get to make decisions, you also have to accept the consequences of that decision. If you want to earn $10,000 dollars in a particular month (quite possible, by the way, if you do the

math), taking two weeks off of work may not be conducive to that achieving that goal. Unless, of course, you are able to find a way to continue working WHILE taking that time off – another idea with considerable possibility when you are in private practice.

I think as helping professionals we are smart enough, and have worked hard enough to have earned the right to call the shots when it comes to our lives and careers. But we often turn that responsibility over to an agency or boss in exchange for the "security" of a regular biweekly paycheck – a concept that is becoming more and more difficult to believe in.

Private practice allows you the autonomy to make your own decisions. With that autonomy comes a new sense of personal responsibility and success. How can you not pass that on to your clients when you work with them? Don't they need and deserve that as much as you do?

Successful

With autonomy and self-responsibility comes the opportunity to define that word for yourself. It is likely going to be different for everyone. Is success a particular dollar amount for you? Is it working in a certain location? Maybe it means accomplishing certain things in your professional life or having time to do the things we want outside of work. When you take responsibility for your career through private practice, it means success is up to you to define, and to achieve.

What a powerful opportunity.
I'm not sure what success means for you, but for me it means making more than I did in an agency and working less time in the office, so that I have more time to spend with my family and the opportunity to work on projects I want to work on.

WORK LESS ± EARN MORE ± INCREASED FAMILY TIME ± NEW VENTURES = SUCCESS

So far, I've been pretty darned successful.

Once you get over the initial shock and fear of entering into your practice and taking responsibility for your professional life, success can come pretty easy. But don't get me wrong, that idea of "taking responsibility" takes time. I spent quite a while just waiting for clients to show up and flood my office, because that's what I was used to. I needed to take responsibility for getting my message out and for letting my community know I was there to help. I had to take responsibility to make sure I was paid in a timely and adequate manner. There was some fear and frustration along the way. But when I truly grasped the idea that I was master of my own professional destiny, things got a lot easier. I am writing this in hopes that you don't have to go through that difficult of a process. I hope that in reading this, you can advance your thinking a few months, or even years, ahead of where I started. Take responsibility. Know that you are in charge when you go into practice.

You are in charge of EVERYTHING. It is a beautiful and scary proposition. I hope the following pages help you to understand how to best take that responsibility.

Authentic
THE word that seems to have the most variation in meaning… I didn't know that it was a business and marketing world buzzword, I really didn't. But I started using that word to describe my beliefs and found that in some venues it is not taken as seriously as I would have it. Hopefully, as therapists, you know what I mean.

We study authenticity and being truly present quite extensively through our graduate work. Being authentic in our world means you get to work with those people whom you are truly called to serve, at the times that work best for both you and them and in a manner that allows you to be fully present. For me, this means working with clients who are truly engaged and invested in their own personal growth and development. It means I get to work with the issues and people that I feel truly and authentically knowledgeable to help – and for those whom I do not have the ability to help, I have a network of other professionals I get to work with and refer to. It means I get to be real and honest with my clients and offer them recommendations that are in their best interest based upon my knowledge and experience, versus offering them recommendations that are in "The Company's" best interest.

Unfortunately, in working with other therapists I have heard too many stories of professionals who were asked to work with client outside their area of expertise or make a recommendation to a client for continued or increase treatment that was more about "The Company's" bottom line, not the client's well-being.

Simply stated, that is just not right. It is also unethical and detrimental to our clients and our profession. In private practice you make the decisions you think are right based upon your knowledge and experience; you work with the clients that are a right fit for you and collaborate with other professionals to ensure that you can refer those who are not a good fit.

In private practice you get to show up for work every day as your authentic self and help your clients find their authentic selves.

"You and I, and all our helping professional friends, in private practice improve our world."

How can it not?
If we are able to take responsibility for our own personal and professional lives, I believe we are able to do better work with our clients. We are able to be truly present with them to empathize with them and to help them in a more genuine manner. When we are not overwhelmed with seeing clients diverse array of issues eight to ten hours a day five days a week – when we are not subjecting ourselves to this kind of burnout, we are able to authentically be with those clients who need us, and whom we are best qualified to help. If we are able to do our best work, we are truly helping people. If we are truly helping people in our area of professional brilliance, they are bound to have a better experience than if they were working with an over-worked therapist on the edge of burnout. When they have a better experience, their lives improve. They may even share about with other people in their lives, and that is passed on. But not only are they sharing about their positive experience, they are able to be more authentically present in their lives. They are able to impact their niche in the world, and that spreads just as much.

When we, as helping professionals, are working in our true brilliance, in our area of expertise, learning to live in abundance versus the world of burnout, we pass these blessings on to our clients both directly and subtly. They know it and feel it, and they get "better."

The best place for us to do that is in private practice.

A Caveat

This is a story about me. These are the events that lead me to where I am today. There is no direct information about starting your private practice here. I am not writing this to inflate my own ego, although the process of recounting these details was very cathartic for me. I am writing this in hopes that you may glean some useful bit of information to use on your journey to your own successful and authentic private practice. I am hopeful that you can gather some ideas in reading this and find ways to avoid the pits I fell in to.

2

My Story

What makes me think I should be writing this book

There are quite a few miss-steps through my story that caused me to end up here, sitting in front of this screen pouring out my passion for private practice to you. To take that many missteps and still find myself able to do this, I call it God, karma, luck, fate, and a whole lot of blessing mixed in. So with all that good fortune pointing me in this direction, I thought I HAD to reach out to share it with you. Let's face it, getting up at 5 A.M. every morning for several month to write is not the action of someone who doesn't feel they MUST reach out to others…

I always loved the field of psychology. I was intrigued by the mystery of trying to figure out the human mind, human behavior, and the plethora of other topics covered in a basic high school psychology course. So it was natural to go on to major in it in college.

Of course, nobody tells you there aren't many jobs available for a Bachelor's Degree in Psychology until AFTER you've paid for the degree or start paying on it.

So I wandered around for a little while. I worked for a growing child & adolescent treatment center near my university, and eventually found that I wanted to help more. I was inspired by the counselors and psychologists who worked there, so I thought it seemed like a good idea to go back to school to study what they studied. I was going to become a Licensed Mental Health Counselor.

I bombed my first admissions application to the grad school program. Miserably.

"What", you might say. "With these incredible writing skills and wit – you didn't get in the first time?!"

That was misstep or **FAILURE No. 1**.

Let's take a moment to salute failure.

> **"** Failure is the universe's way of saying "that probably wasn't a good idea", or "maybe it was a good idea with poor execution."

Failure, I salute you. Thank you for all you have done for me.

That's right, embrace it. Feel it. Taste it. Experience it with all your senses.

What has been your biggest failure thus far in life? What about the next three biggest failures?

My goal for you, if I may be so bold as to set a goal for you, is to avoid THAT particular failure again. Maybe even avoid that level of failure. But I hope you fail again. Not as big as your "biggest" failure. But you should certainly have lots of little ones.

Failure is the universe's way of saying "that probably wasn't a good idea", or "maybe it was a good idea with poor execution". Either way, there's something to learn from it. With each failure in life, there is a valuable lesson, or a ton of valuable lessons, to be learned. The bigger the failure, the more to learn. That is how it has played out in my life.

I have had a few doozies. That +$1,000,000 one I was telling you about earlier; there was this marketing & community outreach idea I poured a bunch of time and money into that only a few people showed up for; my last counseling website… I could easily keep going. Each one was a frustrating, disappointing, expensive, and time-consuming failure.

I learned volumes from each one that I only would have read about in a book or on a website. I was able to experience the work, the emotion, and the outcome in a way that reading about it would not have allowed – that is how true learning took place for me.

Failure is not permanent, as long as you get back up after. The only permanent failure is not to try again.

Now, you can feel frustrated, angry, and down-right depressed after a failure – and you are entitled to feel that way for as long as you want; but I am telling you, it is much better when you get back up, assess your losses, learn your lesson, and move on to success.

It can really be that easy.

I didn't get in to grad school my first time around. I worked and moved up the ladder at the juvenile treatment center I was working at. I got a good taste of money and a small dose of the exhilaration of corporate advancement during that time, but I got a better taste for wanting to go to grad school. So I applied again, learned from the past failure, and got in.

I was pumped, I was excited, I was going to become a world changer and a people-helper! I was feeling groovy.

First class, first night, first words:
"If you are here to make money, you might as well get out"…

WHAT?!

Now, I knew the stories of the "Noble Poor" social worker; and I knew this wasn't a "Get Rich" kind of occupation, but you mean to tell me I just wrapped up four years of student loans (five for me – I REALLY liked undergrad), and I am signing on for two more years, NOT TO MAKE ANY MONEY?!

It was disheartening to say the least. As you may be able to deduce, there wasn't much discussion of how to own or operate a private practice business, or do anything financially significant, in this program. I learned the basics of counseling from a darn good school and program, so that I could go out and work for an agency helping people. Like most of us, I was excited to go out and "Save the World", and I learned a lot about how to do that. But I also was indoctrinated into the idea that it was going to be a financially difficult situation, and that I should be aware of, plan for, and accept the inevitability of the dreaded "burnout"; at which time I should plan to get over it, take whatever meager vacation I was given by my agency, and get back to helping people… Does this sound familiar? Have you been there?

Despite the dismal outlook, I was still excited to get out of school and go *"Save the World."*

So I did. I was very fortunate that the treatment center I was working for was expanding. I was slated to open the Outpatient Counseling department through my internship. My focus was to work with those children and adolescents who were adjudicated to be "delinquent" or "incorrigible," but not so much that they required to be placed in treatment. This is not what you would call an open, honest, and willing caseload.

This was also my first experience in the true family-systems theory, and the idea that "the apple doesn't fall far from the tree". It's pretty hard to convince a 13-year-old kid to decrease, or stop, his marijuana use when mom and dad are supplying or using with him. It was disheartening, but I kept trying.

Eventually, it was time to move on from the safety and security of life in a college town and in to "The Real World." I interviewed at a variety of places "in the big city" and fell in love with the treatment modality and philosophy of a long-term, intensive, adolescent drug-treatment center that worked with the substance dependent adolescent directly and involved the adolescent's family in a very unique way.

I was hooked. I spent two weeks begging the director at that time to hire me. Eventually, he did. And then he quit less than a month later – how is that for helping you feel secure in a new job?

It was an interesting ride, those years there. I spent hours and hours facilitating therapy groups, working with individual clients and their families, and doing more groups. I was also introduced to the exciting adventure of "being

on call" and "crisis intervention."
Forty-hour work weeks easily became 45- or 50-hour ones. The needs of the clients and families had me working until 9 P.M. most Monday's. On Fridays, I was scheduled to 10 P.M. Or, if things got a little crisis-oriented, as they often tended to do at the end of the week, it was 11 P.M. or sometimes midnight. This was not always good for a young therapist and his young wife and family. But the needs of the client and the organization came first.

It was an interesting operation. I enjoyed the work, if not the hours, but felt like there might be something else calling me. After coming out of a very well-funded community mental health center, non-profit work with its second-hand furniture and hand-me-down office equipment was a little difficult to accept. But I stayed on and sought to improve the treatment and the outcomes for that facility.

I eventually fell into the belief that the only way to make any "real" money and to forge a better life for my family was to move into management. Of course, as most mental health agencies do, they convince good therapists that they would make good managers of therapists, and then the game is afoot.

I went that route and learned quickly that being a good manager was different than being a good therapist – a lot of the same skills, attitudes, and ideas were involved, but the demands were significantly different.

The demands were pretty demanding. It was not an easy jump from therapeutic thinking to managerial thinking, at least not for me. The demands on my time increased mightily, and the stress was fairly significant. I was trained to believe that the financial success of my little operation was entirely in my hands, although often I felt like my hands were tied. Have you been there? I'm fairly certain I never took a management business class throughout my entire college career…. It was a daunting and stressful task to take on the responsibility for the success of the site with education in Jungian theory and Cognitive Behavioral techniques. They don't really "fit" very well.

I was quickly learning that, even though clinical management yielded a somewhat better paycheck every two weeks, it was not forging a better life for my family, not with me being at the office even more each week, and having to be gone for days at a time when I had to travel to different sites.

I pushed myself through it for several years. I learned a lot about myself, business, marketing, and just how much stress a body and mind could take. There were times I think I excelled at it. I was asked to do some pretty exciting things through my work there. I spoke on several national talk shows, worked with the Office of National Drug Control Policy, and I worked with local, state, and national news shows – it was quite an honor to do these things. I was somewhat awe struck with the opportunities.

However, the stress continued to build. Burnout was quickly approaching; I was recognizing all of the symptoms we learn about in grad school.
How does a manager best deal with stress and potential burnout? "You push through it!" And, most likely, add to it.

I did.

The funny thing was, despite all the work I was doing and stress I was under for the agency, I still wasn't feeling fulfilled. Not personally, not financially. That's where the million dollar FAILURE begins.

I was the program director, I had heard sweet whispers of "someday, you might be CEO", but I still wanted more. Did it have something to do with the fact that I wasn't really leading an authentic life as a person or as a "therapist"? Was it because I wasn't fulfilled, so I thought that acquisition of more money would do it?

I will let you judge.

The circumstances were right; it was the perfect storm. I was introduced to the idea and opportunity of real-estate investing. This was "the only way" to build a future for my young, growing family. With my wife's support, despite the stress she was feeling from my stress, we jumped on-board. We quickly and easily amassed over a million dollars in rental property within 12 to 18 months.

Now I was program director and head of my own real-estate investing company – I had the responsibility for the success of my treatment center, AND the success of our family real-estate situation. Failure was imminent. I was working 40 to 50 hours at the office, coming home, sometimes stopping to say "hello," and going right into our home office (a corner of our bedroom – another bad idea) to work for three to four hours each night on our real-estate. On the weekends I was out repairing properties or trying to fill vacancies. I developed a fight-or-flight response to the ringing of my cell-phone. It was permanently attached to my waist. If it wasn't tenants calling, it was staff. If it wasn't staff, it was the parent of a client. If it was them, it was the CEO. I didn't have enough ringtones to change through so that my heart didn't race every time it rang.

After a few years of this – rationalizing it was "the only way" to do what was right for my family, it all gave out. It may have been the stress. It may have been good fortune. It could have been a blessing and a wake-up call from God – whatever you want to call it – with quite a bit of drama, I was hospitalized with a ruptured appendix.

I was hospitalized for 10 days, and had two weeks of recovery at home. I learned more about myself and my calling in those 25 days than I had in the previous years leading up to it.

It had to stop. I couldn't keep going like this. Things had to change. They did. I had to make some hard decisions – it eventually became a battle for my health and family versus my job.

My family won, thankfully. I eventually decided to start living a healthier life and started running. I left the company and we moved. We got rid of all the real-estate (and not in the "make-money easy" way of getting rid of it), and I eventually went to work for another agency as a therapist.

Management wasn't for me, neither was the pursuit of "untold riches" in real-estate investing. Stress wasn't for me any more either.

It was amazing how much healthier I felt – mentally, emotionally, spiritually, and physically – when I let my body and mind recover from that stress. I became a better person and a better helping professional.

I learned quite a bit through those years and that FAILURE. It is part of who I am today, and I wouldn't trade it for better times. I am thankful I went through it.

It was the most terrible experience I could ever have imagined while I was going through it though.

Clinical management wasn't for me. If management is the place for you, I am very happy for you. You learned to do what I couldn't. I am certain you make your agency a better place for having figured that out.

However, I would assume that if you are reading this; if you took the time to invest in it, management wasn't or isn't the place for you.

Neither is working for somebody else or for an agency.

As I transitioned out of the area we were living and into another job, I thought I wanted to go into private practice. I thought I was ready. I found that I wasn't and that I had no idea what I was doing.

I interviewed with several clinicians in our new area. I found a variety of opportunities:
> rent an office do your own marketing, billing, and collecting
> fee split with someone else does the bill and some marketing
> fee split where you get a smaller portion, but they do all the other work; billing, marketing, maintenance, cleaning, etc. This can also be called "agency work".

I took the easy way, the last choice. I took the route that guaranteed me clients and no responsibility other than therapy. The agency even did all my insurance set-up! However, it wasn't long before I realized that receiving 45 percent of public-assisted insurance for 80 percent of my caseload was NOT going to pay the bills, even IF I was scheduling clients eight to 10 hours a day, five days each week…. I was being overworked and underpaid, at least for my standards.

But it was "the easy way." The way of no responsibility.

The easy way wasn't so easy. Working for someone else put me close to (more) financial ruin. And I still didn't have the amount of time I wanted with my family or for myself. The decision to go into private practice started out as a necessity. It quickly became a passion.

It took a lot of hard work to get ready to open my practice. But it was fun and enjoyable work because it was working towards something that felt truly authentic, that helps others and that I really wanted to do.

Once the hard-work part was complete, I started figuring out my systems to maintain everything. Those systems have been working pretty well for the past few years. I love the days I go to work and help people I am truly passionate about helping. I enjoy my sales and marketing work. I really like the community outreach work I get to do. Most importantly, I have the time and resources to do those things I am most passionate about: spend time with my family, build relationships in my community, and help others.

That is what puts my before screen today. I am passionate about helping. I am passionate about helping you avoid the pitfalls I fell in to. I am passionate about you starting your own successful and authentic private practice. I am passionate about you feeling as blessed as I feel every day. I am passionate about connecting with you to find out how we continue to help our communities in new and innovative ways.

It feels pretty darn good to feel this passionate about what I am called to do every day. I might even say it feels authentic.

I hope that story resonates with you somewhere, in some way. Although I didn't write with intent to be self-aggrandizing, it feels pretty good to look back on what I have accomplished.

I hope that it helps you accomplish more. I hope something in this book allows you to take your practice and our profession to heights we never imagined.

3

The Business of Building A Private Practice

My approach to building a private practice breaks down into three main categories:

Business – The nuts and bolts. The dollar signs and decimals points – all those things they didn't teach you in graduate school. I will teach you how to maintain your therapist identity while being a business person and how to authentically combine the two in a way that feels right to you.

Marketing – This is when you tell everyone what you are doing so that they send you clients. There are a quite a few ways to do this successfully, and just as many unsuccessful ways. In this section I will offer you a variety of ways to find your unique way of engaging in these necessary behaviors in a way that feels authentic to you. This section should have a ton of ideas you throw out and say, "Not for me!" and just enough that you can grasp, utilize, and make your own.

Personal – You are starting a business. In this business, YOU are the primary product. You are the president and CEO and you are the trash person and head toilet cleaner, and everything in between. As the primary product, there are some ways you can polish and shine the production process, and the end result. I offer my suggestions here.

Your Private Practice – Your Business

Just like any expedition in life, there really is no one "perfect" way to do this. There are a lot of suggestions, good ideas, and ways to do it that might be better than others. You can find quite a bit of information out there on how to go about building your practice – I appreciate the fact that you trust me enough to invest in this particular way to do it. You may find different books and experts representing different ways to do it. Some will claim theirs is the only way to do it. I'm here to tell you that there are many ways to go about achieving your goal, all of which may be right.

The only WRONG way to go about it is not to go about it at all.
I take that back, there are A LOT of wrong ways to go about it – but most are unethical – I am operating from the assumption that you are a caring and ethical person.

The biggest WRONG step you could take is not to do anything at all. It is almost too easy to get wrapped up in the paralysis of analysis. You could spend a lifetime researching just the right way to start thinking about maybe getting to the possibility of writing a plan to maybe start your practice… There is a lot of information out there, but you don't have to read it all. But what you DO have to do to get started is to get started. We need you out there doing your best work, so get to it.

The goal of this section is to provide a comprehensive review of the business minded decisions you need to make and the actions you have to take to get on the path to a successful and authentic private practice. These are decisions that need to be made starting out, and just about every year you are in practice.

There really isn't a linear path to making these decisions. Some will naturally come before other, like determining where you are going to practice so that you can have an address and phone number before you start making business cards. As I think about, that's not even an absolute… You could easily have a card with a website ready to go before a phone, address, and physical location… Like I said there are few absolutes, just some ideas that are better than others – that work better than others. Determine your path with the advice given here, and start moving.

These are the business areas that require your attention. These are the details surrounding those decisions. I recommend keeping a journal, or a notebook, or even a Word document to start writing down your thoughts and plans around these ideas. I still find my original notes and documents provide an interesting source of ideas and inspiration even today.

The Business Mindset
The first, most important, absolutely necessary business mindset to adopt – that I hope you have already adopted – is that TIME AND MONEY are your two most valuable commodities and assets. Please note that time is first and definitely the most important. As a business-person, you need to respect, appreciate, defend, and manage both to the best of your ability. Too often, as helping professionals we do not value our own time. In business – in the business of you and your authentic private practice – time is money. Money is the lifeblood that allows your practice to keep going to help more people. Not managing the relationship between time and money is the death knell of many private practices. Learn how the two relate in your personal and professional life and leverage them to be the best person and professional you can be.

You don't have to have your MBA to run a successful private practice (it would be an interesting combo if you did!), but you do have to think like a businessperson; I would even go a step further a say you should start thinking like an entrepreneur. In my mind, an entrepreneur is a "business person with a ton of creativity." And as you and I both know, therapists, social workers, counselors, and psychologists naturally have a ton of creativity – so you are already halfway there. It's just adding the "business" aspect to that creativity.
In fact, if I may be so bold to go a step further, I really think helping professional are one of the MOST well-suited and well-prepared groups of people to run their own business.

As I have read and researched business and marketing over the years, the BIG ideas have really remained the same, it's the details that change. One of those BIG ideas, one of the main concepts of running an effective and profitable business is the idea of CONNECTING with your customer, building rapport, and investing in a relationship with your customer.

Connecting, building rapport, showing empathy, joining with our client; aren't these the BIG ideas we were taught, trained in, and completed research on all throughout our education?! Isn't that what we do on a daily basis in working with our clients? Are we not masters and doctors in rapport and connecting with our "customer"?

I think we are.

You might be amazed to hear how much training and education business, sales, and marketing folk have to go through to get to where you are naturally and through your studies when it comes to connecting. You, as a helping professional eat, breathe, sleep, and live connecting with others. You are a natural connector, and you have honed that natural trait through years of study. You are already creative, and you are a natural connector. With these two traits you are well on your way to a successful and authentic private practice! All you need to do is learn to adapt that training, education, and experience in a more business-focused manner. You already build therapeutic rapport with your clients. Now build rapport and connection with your referral sources and your community. You already share brilliantly transformative ideas with your clients in session; now share those same concepts with potential clients in your marketing and website design.

It is not a huge transformation for a helping professional to go from effective therapist in an agency or community mental health center to outstanding, successful, and authentic professional in private practice.

You have what it takes. You were trained for this. You have the experience you need. If you are reading this, I feel pretty safe in assuming you are ready for it.

My only concern, the BIG thing that might hold you back is how you were trained to relate to MONEY. That's right, money – that thing we were told not to expect in our work.

If you are going to run a business, you have to be comfortable with money. If you want to keep your business open for years to come, helping more and more people, you need to generate a PROFIT from your business. If you want to continue to grow your business, to help more people in more effective and generous ways, you are going to have to generate MONEY to be able to do this. In order to generate money – in order to make a profit, you are going to have to learn to ask for it. It will not fall out of the sky.

How do you feel about money? Do you embrace it as a resource to help you, your family, your business, and your client; or do you shy away from it? What would you do if you had all the money you needed?

Would you take more vacation time, so that you were more refreshed, relaxed, and re-energized when you met with your clients?

Would you offer a more comfortable and calming atmosphere for your clients in your office and waiting area, so that they came to session relaxed and ready to do the difficult work involved in therapy?

Would you invest more in your own personal growth and development as a helping profession and as a person, so that you could be a greater asset to your community?

What would you do? How would that feel? What would it look like? How can you get there?

It starts with being comfortable with money.

Money is not good or bad. Money IS. We place subjective judgments - good, bad, right, wrong – upon it. Money is a resource, just like time. What we choose to do with it is positive or negative.

What are your attitudes towards money? Were you taught that it is the root of all evil and to be avoided, or are you ready to embrace it as a resource to help yourself, your family, your clients, and your community?

Are you ready to start asking your clients to pay you a fair and honest rate for your services? If not, you may have some work to do with being able to ask your clients for their co pay, or full-fee payment. Know that you will have to seek out paying clients to keep your business alive and vibrant. Plan to set a fair fee for yourself and your clients.

What does it mean for you to be paid well and how does that relate to your clients? This is one of the first important questions for you to answer as you begin the journey to your successful and authentic private practice.
I also want to encourage you, as you start thinking more like a business-person, more like an entrepreneur, and to start thinking about where you can

build that knowledge and education. Just as we continue to invest in CEU's and professional development as therapists, it is important to continue to learn and grow as an entrepreneur.

If you have read my previous articles, you know I am a huge fan of Seth Godin and his body of work. In one of his latest books, Linchpin, he shared extensively about the idea of doing "emotional labor". Is there a business concept that is anywhere closer to what we do every day? I think not – check out Linchpin, or subscribe to his blog at www.SethGodin.com. You may have also read my thoughts on artist Hugh Macleod. I get an insightful chuckle out of his daily comics from www.gapingvoid.com ; the last book of his I read, Ignore Everybody and 39 Other Keys to Creativity was full of great success stories and ideas. His second book Evil Plans, reads like it was written for therapists in private practice! I also subscribe to several innovative business magazines; Fast Company and Entrepreneur being the top two. I read quite a few blogs every week. Chris Brogan, www.ChrisBrogan.com , puts out several articles on several different topics each week. I love his work. Chris Guillebeau writes The Art of Non-Conformity several times each week at www.ChrisGuillebeau.com .

You don't have to read any of these, or you could read all of them. The bottom line is to start seeking out opportunities to improve your thinking about business, marketing, and sales. You must learn to think outside your naturally brilliant therapist mind and step outside your comfort zone, just like you ask your clients to do. These authors have offered me more information and guidance over the past few years that I have been reading them, than I am able to summarize in these few pages. Find your "business muse": the people or person (I recommend more than one to get a diversity of ideas) that inspire you to grow outside of what you already know or think you know about business – it will help you more than you know.

Location

Choosing a location can be a very stressful part of starting a private practice; it can also be as simple as answering a few questions.

Where do you want to practice? What location is going to help you build your business quicker and more effectively? Personally, I not so sure this question is as important as we might think it is. It is a question that needs to be answered, of course. But I don't think THIS is the one to lose any sleep over.

Your biggest question might just be "What is available to get started?"
You are going to want to locate your practice to close proximity to your target market. Assumedly, your target market is nearby, and you are not going to travel more than 50 miles each day to have to get to work.

For me, that's a real sticking point, but it may be different for you. After years of grande-commutes for previous employers, the idea of traveling more than 10 miles to get to my office just wears me out. I don't want to do it. A local commute keeps me fresh and helps me to avoid burnout. That may be different for you. Either way, I don't recommend having to travel too far, or have to stay over-night to work in your office. Waking up on your office couch and walking to your desk to start seeing your first clients just doesn't seem right. On the other hand, there are plenty of therapists out there who have additions or areas in their own home where they hold their sessions, and many have been very successful at it. With the ever increasing presence of internet technology and social media, it is possible to operate a successful practice without even having an office. You can find out more about the world of online therapy from Kate Anthony and Deanna Merz Nagel in their book, Therapy Online: A Practical Guide.

Other factors to consider are the decision to rent or buy, and whether or not you want to work as part of a group, or go solo. Unless you've got a cache of extra cash stored away, or an extra building in the vicinity of the location where you want your office to be, you will likely be renting at first. You might even consider just sub-leasing for a few days each week while you build your caseload. You may or may not want to go in with a group or a few other therapists to save on costs. These decisions are really based on your personal needs. Just keep in mind how they will relate to your business needs.
The bottom line for selecting your location is to make it someplace where YOU want to go, and a place your clients will feel safe and comfortable going to. Consider the strategic selection of your location as it relates to your target audience. If possible, select your site with ease-of-access for your ideal client in mind.

When it comes to making your office comfortable, aside from overall location, furnishings would be the next most impactful topic. There are a few areas to consider: the front entry, waiting room, your office, and your restroom.

Your office, the place where you conduct your sessions, the place where the work is done, should be a place where clients can feel comfortable and at ease in order to work with you. Furnishings should be clean, and relatively new appearing – you don't want to utilize worn and threadbare hand-me-downs if you are going to ask your clients to pay cash. Investing a small amount in your furnishings will go a long way in presenting a particular image. Comfortable couches, loveseats, and straight-back chairs are usually the recommended fair. Portable office chairs or up-scale desk chairs are helpful if you have to add seating for bigger family sessions. I also encourage a little bit of decoration – something on the walls to make for that comfortable feeling – for some reason, sparse white walls seem just a little too "institutional" and not conducive to clients getting comfortable to do the work they need to do.

Here is an example, my office: enough seating for a couple or an individual to choose (*it's interesting how once they make that first decision at intake, it rarely changes in later sessions!*) and then some extra seats at my desk and beyond to bring in if I need more. You can also see that I do some play therapy and a lot of reading in my office. No, I don't read with the clients, but I do recommend books from that shelf.

The waiting area should be of similar comfort. As you can see, mine is a bit of a living room with the couches and coffee table in the middle, and the extra

seating or "office seating" around the outside. We have plenty to read in case clients get their early, toys for children to play with, and some soft music playing in the background. Going in to each office is a white noise machine in order to maintain confidentiality.

Most importantly, my office and the waiting area are clean, organized, smell nice, and are welcoming to my clients. This should be the same for the restroom. Your clients are going to use it at some point on the way in to session or after. It will leave an impression, make sure it is the impression you want. I think that is really the overall message. Just as when we go in to a doctor's office, a restaurant, a place of business, or someone's home, the experience tells us a myriad of details about the people or person there, your office will tell your clients a myriad about you. I think the most obvious question it will answer for your clients is, "Can this person help me?" If your office is scattered, cluttered, dirty, and tattered, but you are trying to help your client get their lives "organized," "cleaned-up," "put-together," etc… well, it just doesn't make sense.

Take pride in your work space. Keep your office and accoutrements organized and clean. Your clients will notice and show their appreciation by continuing to work with you, and by referring their friends.

On Location and Decor
Long ago, before I had my own office, I worked in several others throughout different locations, most of which were quite a distance away from where my office is now. When I discontinued practice at those other locations, several clients opted to drive to my new office to continue work with me, rather than change therapists at the current site, despite the significantly longer drive. I had invested quite a bit of time and effort (and the goodwill of my partners, as they were there before me and did much of the work first) in to the new space, the transfer clients noticed the difference. Several of them commented, "I would gladly make the drive and sit in this waiting room over the previous one." You can gain or lose clients simply on what you offer them to sit in, and the atmosphere of your office – you are EXPERT in human emotions and behavior, use that expertise when setting up your office. It doesn't take long to form an opinion of a person – if you have read Malcolm Gladwell's BLINK you know that the cliché "It only takes seven seconds to make a first impression" is fairly accurate – use that time wisely when it comes to setting up your office.

*Side-note: **MEN** (and I can say this as I am one of you) GET A WOMAN'S TOUCH in your office!

I could never have had my office look as nice as it does without my female partners and my wife's inspection. There is just something about what they notice that we do not. Enlist the help of a female partner, peer, friend or spouse when it comes to picking out the furniture, decorations, and putting it all together. I have been to far too many male therapists' offices to find a desk chair, a plastic office chair, and a light switch… Yes, we can work our trade just about anywhere, but if you are going to have an office, invest and take pride in it! It will pay dividends.

Name

This is a fairly easy decision: do you want to use your professional name or a more descriptive phrase related to your practice? A New Direction Counseling is as much a reflection of me as it is my counseling style – I chose that name with various logo ideas, business cards, and other concepts in mind. Some days I wish I hadn't – it's a devil to cram in to some small typing or writing spaces – 23 letters are costly when it comes to signage. However, it makes for a heck of a cool logo, and I think it gives a fairly direct message to my clients or potential clients.

Choose wisely. When you decide to go with your name, or a business name, you will want to stick with it – changing the name under which you do business is not easy six to 12 months into practice – this name will be in phone books, on marketing material, business cards, websites, office signage, letterhead, etc. Choose wisely. Think professionally.

Take some time to think about it – do the appropriate searches for website domain names and other businesses with similar names in your state. Grow into the name and then take it as yours – unless you use your name, and then it already is yours.

As you name your business, you will want to consider how that relates to the name of your website, or its URL – they don't have to be the same. I originally started with my business name and URL being the same. A New Direction Counseling was found as www.ANewDirectionCounseling.com. However, as I plan my second redesign of the site, I am considering using more search engine optimization (SEO) helpful terms. Words that will help me get noticed by the internet search engines a bit more readily. This is definitely an idea to talk to your web person about.

Licenses

I am taking for granted that you have a license to practice in your state. Or, at the very least, you have a temporary license as a newer graduate that allows you to practice in your state and bill insurance companies. These details and letters after your name vary from state to state, although most are similar in that they require 2,000 hours, or about two years of supervised work after graduation, and then a test to earn your LPC, or LMHC, or LCSW, or whatever license your state gives you – therefore I am writing as if you have already accomplished this.

When it comes to the idea of a "business license" – each community varies even more than the states do. This is something you are going to have to research with the community you plan to practice in. Do no start planning your business until you factor in your need for a business license. This is usually as easy as going to your local chamber of commerce, city zoning commissioner, or whatever agency you may have. Check with businesses in the proximity of where you want to practice, search online, and find out what kind of licenses you need for your area to open your business.

Insurance

This tends to be THE BIG QUESTION for many helping professionals – are you going to accept insurance or not? It is an important question to ask yourself regularly, once you are in practice. But it is a particularly important question to answer in the beginning stages of your practice. Although it is easy to get stressed about this question, it really can be a fun one to deal with because it directly relates to how much you would like to make, in connection with how you would like to work.

Just like everything else that is not of a black and white ethical nature in our field, the answer this question can be just as murky. I see it being a lot like the old, "What theory are you?" "I'm eclectic", discussion when you got out of grad school and thought you had to answer that with The One True Theory. You may have found that there is no one true theory; but a variety of concepts, techniques, and ideas that work for different people.

The great insurance debate is the same mixed bag of eclecticism. There are a myriad of ways to handle it that can benefit you, your clients, and your business.

Here are the facts as I know them, have experienced them, and have seen or helped others with them:

Accepting Insurance –sometimes it can be a great big hassle, sometimes it's pretty wonderful.

HASSLES:
- Preauthorization calls
- Continuing authorization calls
- Non-payment because you mistakenly exceeded authorization
- Waiting to be paid
- Low reimbursement rates
- Writing-filing-sending claims
- Delayed gratification.

NOT HASSLES:
- Co pays
- Getting the mail and feeling like it's Christmas because the big insurance company finally paid you for two months of seeing six clients
- Connecting with the insurance authorization person on the phone and realizing they don't like doing this any more than you do
- Calling for authorization and finding out that the client doesn't need authorization
- Not having to explain for the seventh time that day why you don't take insurance even though the big community mental health agency down the road does even though you provide better service
- Knowing you can help more people.

It can go either way. As for me, I am an insurance eclectic. I accept some insurance, not all, and I accept a reasonable rate for fee-for-service.

I've been doing this long enough to know that there are several insurance companies that are easy to work with, pay in a timely manner, aren't a hassle to deal with, and pay relatively well. I choose to work with those insurance companies, some of which are just as easy as, or easier than, direct billing the client.

There are those insurance companies out there who are a HUGE hassle to work with, rude, untimely, have a lot of red tape, and don't pay well. I don't work with those insurance companies. The interesting phenomenon is this – those clients who have those insurance companies understand! Usually they have encountered enough difficulty with their insurance company that they understand why I wouldn't be in network or accept their insurance. From that understanding, we are able to negotiate a fair rate (usually my normal rate, unless they qualify for a reduced fee per my participation in the National Health Service Corps).

I have also worked with clients who simply don't want to use their insurance for various other reasons. Usually because they understand how wide-open their records become, and sometimes simply because they know the hassle. Of course, as our economy changes, there are more and more people who simply have catastrophic coverage with a $5,000 deductible or higher. They are usually going to be used to paying full-fee for service and will understand the process.

As you can see, there are quite a few variables to consider – mostly outside your control – most of which are related to who your clients are and what insurance companies are most prevalent in your area of your state.
What is yours to control is whether or not you accept insurance, and which insurance companies you will choose to work with if you do.

If you are just starting out in private practice, or are still forming your reputation, I think accepting insurance is the way to go, AS LONG AS YOU GO ABOUT IT STRATEGICALLY AND AUTHENTICALLY. You have to take the time for figure out what insurance companies are willing to allow you to do the work you do best, and which ones you can work with without allowing them to suck the empathy right out of you.

There are several strategies to do this:
Start the CAQH process – Most of us have heard of it, but aren't quite sure what it is. Even though the process, and the six-month updates, can be quite the pain in the neck, it really is fairly helpful.

CAQH stands for the *Council for Affordable Quality Healthcare*; you can find them at *www.CAQH.org*. Basically, they are a clearinghouse and verification service for insurance companies. You take the time to enter in all your personal and professional information, they hold on to it and update it with you every six months, and then share it with the insurance companies you want them to – you get to select where the information goes. The good part is that you enter your data once in to your system, and then if you sign contracts with multiple insurance companies, they can get your info from CAQH, rather than having you have to go through the arduous process multiple times. Most states are mandating that insurance companies in their state work with CAQH, so it makes sense to take the time to be a part of it if you think you are going to accept insurance.

It takes time to complete this process. If you think you are interested in accepting insurance, start the CAQH process immediately! I believe the current estimate is three to six months from start to finish. Keep in mind that is just for CAQH, then you have to contract with the insurance companies. The entire process from starting CAQH to completed contract with insurance company can take six to 12 months.

Get your National Provider Identifier (NPI) – The National Health and Human Services website (www.hhs.gov) defines the NPI as follows:

The National Provider Identifier (NPI) is a Health Insurance Portability and Accountability Act (HIPAA) Administrative Simplification Standard. The NPI is a unique identification number for covered health care providers. Covered health care providers and all health plans and health care clearinghouses must use the NPIs in the administrative and financial transactions adopted under HIPAA. The NPI is a 10-position, intelligence-free numeric identifier (10-digit number). This means that the numbers do not carry other information about healthcare providers, such as the state in which they live or their medical specialty. The NPI must be used in lieu of legacy provider identifiers in the HIPAA standards transactions.

You can apply or update your NPI and related information at The National Plan & Provider Enumeration System (NPPES) or go to https://nppes.cms.hhs.gov/NPPES/StaticForward.do?forward=static.npistart to get started.

Basically your NPI number is your practitioner "social security number" – you need it to do just about anything related to insurance, as that is how they identify you. When you bill an insurance company, you need your NPI placed in a variety of blanks – go get one if you are going to accept insurance.

If you have been in the field for a while, if you have worked for an agency or any group that has billed for services using your name, you are likely to already have an NPI number. If any entity is billed using your information, they had to have your NPI number. Check with that agency or the NPPES to get it. If you are just starting out, you should expect to have to file for your number. Now, start shopping for insurance companies. That's right, you are shopping for them, not the other way around. You get to choose who you work with – and that includes insurance companies, if you choose to do so.

Some of the insurance company strategies I used starting out:

> **Find out who the "Big Providers" are in your area** – what insurance do the schools, hospitals, and larger factories carry? Are they accepting new providers? If you accept the primary insurance of a 500-employee hospital, you would think it should be pretty easy to accept four to five clients, right? Repeat that with a few employers in your area and you're close to a full caseload.
> *NOTE: this turns in to an obvious marketing strategy. If you accept the insurance for the local schools, isn't it a good idea to go introduce yourself to the school counselor and ask if you can be of service to the teachers, administration, students, or parents? If you are in-network with the insurance company that services the biggest factory in town, shouldn't you introduce yourself to their human resources department and anyone else who will speak to you?)
> **Look online** – see who the insurance providers are in your state, city, or town – go through their provider section to review rates, or request a rate sheet and look at their contract structure.
> **Call the provider relations representative for your area** – these are the gatekeepers to contracts and rate sheets – give them a call and strike up a conversation! Most are more than happy to help! It's their job. It is what they are there to do.
> **Look into the Employee Assistance Program (EAP) providers in your area** – most major manufacturing companies and their subsidiaries offer some kind of EAP assistance to their employees – do the research to find out if you want to be one of their providers. Historically, EAPs offer low reimbursement rates, but many referrals; you have to ask yourself if that is how you want to work.
> **Finally NEGOTIATE, NEGOTIATE, NEGOTIATE!!!** Before you sign

that contract, ask for a better rate. It's as simple as that. Know what your fee-for-service rate is and ask for it; the worst they can say is "No thank you".

I can tell you from my experiences, most EAPs have some negotiating room. That's because they offer you the lowest hourly rate available, and can move up from there! EAP negotiating is as simple as stating, "I would like X dollars" to your representative, they will give you the used car salesman speech, "let me talk to my manager and get back to you", and then you go back and forth like that for a few days until either they can't budge and you won't accept it, or they can't budge and you do accept it. Again – it is your choice – YOU CHOOSE WHO YOU WORK WITH AND WHAT INSURANCE YOU TAKE.

An Insurance / EAP story
I once "accidentally" accepted a contracted rate from an EAP. It was for a client who was transferring from a previous agency where I saw him, and it was somewhat of a favor to work with the EAP to be able to see him. I did the work, signed the contract, and worked with him for several sessions. Of course, I was two to three sessions in before the EOBs and payments started showing up – at a rate of $30 per hour!?!?!?!

I was not too pleased, so I called the number on the EOB, went through phone system, and asked a human being to change my contracted rate or terminate the contract. We went through the aforementioned process, and they eventually settled on $60 per session – below my normal rate, but again, it was a favor for this particular client, so I accepted. Unfortunately, that process has turned me off to working with any other EAPs.

The REALLY FRUSTATING part, the part that still steams me today - when I was seeing him at the previous agency, I was contracted with them for 45 percent of that $30 rate… $13.50 per session… My blood still boils thinking about it. Hence, my somewhat biased disposition against EAPs and working for other people who may not be giving you a fair deal….

Speaking of fair deal, back to the idea of negotiating your rate with insurance companies. EAPs and small, local insurance companies are usually open to negotiation and debate. If you have a fair rate that is comparable to other local providers, they will usually work to meet you close to it.

On the other hand, larger insurance companies simply won't. They have the leverage in the relationship. When looking at contracting with larger insurance companies, you can try to negotiate, but more than likely, you will simply accept or not accept their rate and contract, and that's OK. You still get to choose. For me, I really like working with Anthem / Blue Cross Blue Shield in my state. They are a fairly no hassle outfit that pays fairly well – a little less than my normal rate, but their timeliness, ease of access, and large market compensate for it, in my opinion.

The bottom line, the BIG message I want you to understand is that you have a CHOICE. You have A LOT of CHOICES! You can choose to accept insurance or not. You can choose what insurance companies and EAPs you want to work with. You can choose what rates you will accept and what ones you will not.

When we think of insurance companies as giant multibillion dollar corporations versus little ol' private practice us, it can be intimidating. When you call and talk to a provider rep, or a case manager, they are people just like you and me. They are able to operate within certain parameters of authorizing treatment and contracting you. Sometimes they don't even like it, but it's what they have to do – you get to choose whether or not you want to work with what they are able to offer. I have found that most of the insurance people I have come in contact with are very helpful and fun to chat with when I approach them with the attitude that I know they are there to help me and my clients. But they can't always help because of the rules of their particular company. In the end, I still get to choose if I want to play by their rules or move on.

So let's talk about what it is like to "Move On".

What if your client doesn't use insurance, or you don't accept their insurance? Simple. You charge them a fair rate, and they pay cash, check, or credit at the end of the session. For me a "fair rate" is comparable to what other practitioners are asking for in my area. I did a little market research, found out what others were charging, and then started billing at a little under that. I was the "new guy," and it helped me bring more clients in faster. Eventually being the new guy wore off, and I increased my rates. It's nice to give yourself a raise from time to time.

Experience and working with other therapists has taught me that "fair rate" usually depends on demographics – location and socio-economic status of your area of practice – which would then relate directly to your cost of living – making for a nice complete cycle. If you have a rural or small-town practice, $75-125 per hour seems to be the norm; suburban goes slightly higher at $90-150, and then urban rates have a greater range from $100-250 or beyond per session.

Why is that helpful to know? Because you deserve to realistically consider your earning potential. It is directly tied to your demographics. Now, you can attempt to go outside those demographics, but it's going to be a heck of a battle. That is just a business fact. You cannot successfully fight the market forces as a one-person operation. When it comes to seeing clients in session, one hour at a time, you are limited to what you can charge and what you can make. AND THAT IS OK!!

Please accept now the reality that our earning in our practices – seeing clients each hour – is bound by where we work and whom we work with. You can make a very good income at this, far better than the "secure income" of agency work, but it is still bound by the rules of the market.

Now, if you choose to work with clients only part of the week, and do "other things" with your free time; relax, write, work, teach, pontificate and ponder; you can always increase that earning potential in an AUTHENTIC manner. I see that as the "new business model" of private practice. But we will have to talk about that another day in another book. Let's get you moving with the foundation – the traditional model – first.

Finances
Start tracking them now. Now that you have adopted a business mindset, money is something to pay attention to and respect. When it comes to business, money is leverage. Money is a resource. It is numbers to be tracked and understood.

It's not really that difficult. I use a simple, free program – Quickbooks – to track my expenses. It gives me the categories to put it in to, and it lets me know how much I've spent on my business in a given amount of time. You can download the latest version free online, or you can use an Excel spreadsheet.

A NOTE ABOUT THE NATIONAL HEALTH SERVICE CORPS

You may have already heard about the NHSC's loan repayment program. You may have already applied to have your student loan repaid, or researched the opportunity. It's been around for quite a while. Unfortunately, I'm betting you haven't heard of it. Sadly, it's been my experience that not many of us know about it.

The National Health Service Corps Loan Repayment Program is an opportunity for mental health practitioners to receive payment on their student loans in exchange for a contracted amount of service with the NHSC ranging from two to six or more years. For TWO YEARS service, you can receive up to $60,000 to pay on your student loans. You can continue your service each year after that for up to six or more years to receive up to $170,000 or complete loan repayment if your loans total over that amount. It's one of those deals I thought was too good to be true, until $50,000 (they raised the payment rates to $60,000 in 2011) was deposited in to my savings account – I wish I still had the picture to show you. That amount was quickly passed on to my student loans, before the ideas of Mexico and a life on the beaches came to fruition! There are a few different ways to go about it. If you work or are working for an agency and planning your practice or group practice that is already authorized and contracted with the NHSC, ask about it. Contracted agencies are encouraged to use this as a retention tool so that good therapists continue to serve.

If you are already in private practice or are close to starting yours – you can have your practice authorized to be a provider of NHSC LRP contracts. It's a bit of a process, but if I can get through it, anyone can. You get your location authorized, and then you sign up as a practitioner of that practice, and *abracadabra* big chunk of loan disappears!

The trade off is the contracted service. You must be practicing in an area deemed "in need" of professionals – you can research it on their website. From the contract, you agree to service Medicaid and Medicare clients as well as offer a sliding fee schedule commensurate with the national poverty guidelines. For me, right now, it means I have to work a little harder to compensate for the pro bono work I do – but it feels good, and seriously, $50,000 ($60,000 for you) to work a little harder over the next two years? No question it was the right decision for me.

If you are interested, check it out at http://nhsc.hrsa.gov/loanrepayment/, or feel free to email me.

TAXES!!! Yes, you are a business owner now. Even if you haven't completely opened shop yet, you need to start tracking those expenses in order to apply for the appropriate deductions and other bonuses when it comes to tax time. The other important reason is in order to conduct an analysis each month and year to see if your business is successful. From that analysis, you can make smart business decisions related to marketing, advertising, and the direction you need to be taking your operations.

Track your numbers, your dollars coming in and out, and chat with your tax professional about what to do with them. Depending on where you are in life, you may have to pay part of your taxes every quarter in order not to have a big payment at the end of the year. If you are used to getting money back at the end of each tax season because you had so much deducted from your agency job each paycheck, that might change. Any way you look at it, consulting with a tax professional is going to give you much more sound advice than I can here.

$$+ \frac{\text{Track your numbers}}{\text{Talk to a tax professional}}$$

Make smart business decisions based on those numbers.

While we are talking about numbers, let's talk about a really fun one – Your Salary.

What is your salary? That's right, you get to choose. This may be the first time in your life YOU get to choose your salary, and YOU have all the power to make that happen within the rules of the market force.

Remember, you MUST pay attention to the prevailing market forces. If you do not, it makes things a lot more difficult.

Here are a few things to think about – a few exercises – to consider when planning your salary. This is based on simple math and market forces.

How much do you want to make?

Here are the variables...

How many clients you are going to see / how many hours you want to work each week

Multipled by

How much you will charge per client

Multipled by

How many weeks you are going to work each year

(Let's face it, you're not getting in to this to have those paltry "two weeks of vacation" your previous employer gave you, are you? You are a helping professional for goodness sakes! You can't be helping others unless you are taking care of yourself, right? So let's just estimate, for the sake of good fun that you are going to take eight weeks off each year and work 44 weeks… ahhh… the sweet life! We'll talk about what you're going to do with those eight weeks later.

EQUALS= YOUR YEARLY SALARY

So let's play around with those numbers a bit.

There seems to be a prevailing thought out there that $100,000 for the year indicates you "made it." So let's take that number, with the most average of average hourly rates factored in – $100 per hour (keep in mind, insurance reimbursement is most likely lower for regular sessions but somewhat higher for intakes).

Let's see… 100,000 for the year at $100 per hour, for 44 weeks means you would need to see around 23 clients each week (22.72 to be exact, but I am not sure you want to see 0.72 of a client, so we'll round up).

You can tweak the numbers from there:

Will your market not support $100 per hour? See a few more clients each week, work a few more weeks, or become comfortable with less than $100,000 for the year.

What if you weren't so worried about making $100,000? What if half of that, $50,000 for the year, was OK with you? You could see half as many clients. You could charge half as much. Or you could work half as many weeks.

Want to make more? Charge more, see more clients, or work more weeks. There are a myriad of possibilities. The bottom line – YOU get to choose. There is a down side, however, even if it has a silver lining.

Expenses
Expenses in private practice are quite a bit more than in the 40-plus-hours-per-week world of working for an agency. You need to consider rent, marketing and advertising expenses, supplies, phone and internet, etc. The silver lining is that these are all tax deductible, and, again, YOU get to choose how or where that money is spent.

Billing
Billing is often considered a necessary evil. It is either a financial expense or a time expense, depending on how you go about it. You will be dedicating some resource, money or time, to it as a business minded therapist.
You can choose to work with a person or company that will do you billing for you. You submit the information for your intakes and sessions, they keep the necessary info and send out your insurance bills or client bills each week, two weeks, or month. Usually around 10 percent of whatever money is paid to you is their salary. I've heard it may be a little more of a little less, depending on where you are.
This is an easy way to get the job done and not have to worry about it yourself. You can usually find billing professionals in your local phone book, newspaper, or with a quick online search.

Hiring out your billing is a quick and effective way to get the job done. It frees up your time at the expense of your money. It can be a blessing or a curse, depending on the person you have doing the work for you. There is the variable of adding another person to the mix of your billing that may slow things down, or speed them up. It really depends on the person or system you use. As for me, I do my own billing. I, quite honestly, enjoy doing it. Every Friday morning I spend an hour or two preparing insurance bills and documenting income. Because I am the one doing it, I feel like I have a stronger connection to the financial lifeblood of my business; I know what claims are going out, what payments have come in, and what authorizations may be coming due. I feel a little safer and in control of where the ship is going when I do my billing. I did have someone else doing it at one time, starting out, and they did a great job. But it seemed I got paid a little bit slower, and it was certainly 10 percent less. Moreover, I was not as connected with my business, which made me feel uncomfortable.

I quickly decided to invest in billing software and to take control of the financial operations of my business. I use software called Shrinkrapt, a program created by a former therapist in Chicago. There are many different options out there. I chose this one because it was recommended by someone I trust; she was using it and had volunteered to spend some time showing me how to use it. If you are fortunate enough to have situation like that, where someone will demonstrate their software, or recommends and will teach you a particular brand, by all means, go with that brand.

Even though it can be a little overwhelming at first, I think taking the time and money to learn to do my own billing was well worth it. The up-front cost was around $500 for the software, which is somewhat on the cheaper side, I believe. Then, of course, there was the initial time investment – I spent about an hour with my peer having her show me the program intricacies. Of course the real-time investment came the first few times I did my billing. I'm sure the first few weeks, it took me more than an hour to do my billing each Friday morning – I'm sure it was closer to two or three hours. And, of course, it was a bit frustrating. It took a while to learn how to actually use the program after I got done cursing it and it's evil friend the printer.

Now that I have been using it for a while, it's a piece of cake. I have my system down, and it runs fairly smoothly.

> **My system with Shrinkrapt goes like this:**
> Enter the initial data the week of the intake
> Call the insurance company to see if authorization is needed
> File in the software
> Hit "print" to bill for session
> Put in envelop and send it out

The software formats all the info so that it fits into the claims form and comes out of my printer. I do have to buy claims forms at the local office supply store, another expense.

Each new session is documented into the software, complete with notes, on my laptop in my office. At the end of the week, I pull up all the session files, hit "print," and ship them off. The system has gotten pretty easy.
In the beginning, it took more time as I learned to navigate the software system and the insurance system. If you are going to do your own billing, prepare for it to take a little bit more time in the beginning in order to learn to navigate the systems. Once you do, use those systems to develop your system of managing your billing and taking control of the financial well-being of your business.

Of course, there is also a third option, and that is to take cash and not do any billing. Which really isn't much of an option, in reality. Even if you accept cash-only, fee-for-service, it is still customary to offer the service of providing your clients with an invoice so that they can bill their insurance company. Of course, you also MUST keep good notes on your clients and their sessions as part of most professionals' ethical codes and licensing requirements. Even if you decide on a "cash-only" practice, there will still be some paperwork to do. Make sure you plan for it.

Hours
This is another one of those fun areas where YOU get to choose. Of course, your choice will be impacted by the nature of the market forces, and you will have positive and negative consequences associated with your choice.
More than likely, if you are coming out of an agency to go in to private practice, you have been working 40 or more hours each week AND splitting some "on-call" time with your peers during the evenings and weekends.

You don't have to do this anymore. In fact, I recommend you DO NOT work 40-plus hours each week anymore or ever again!

It is very important to start to consider your professional boundaries as you go in to practice, or restructure the one you have. No longer is it necessary to see eight to 10 clients back-to-back five days each week. Quite honestly, the popular opinion among practitioners is that somewhere around 20 client hours (plus or minus five) is a good number to be financially stable, and, most importantly, mentally and emotionally healthy for your own practice.
Of course, there is still the marketing and operations time you need to put in. There is a direct relationship between clients being seen and marketing time; if you are not seeing clients, you should be dreaming up and acting upon your

marketing plans.

The act of setting your hours is more than just a business practice, but it cuts to the very core of your personal professional boundaries. Nothing sets you up more for failure or success than how you respect or disrespect your own boundaries. You may have learned through your work with other people or agencies not to respect your own time. If you carry this belief into private practice, you will quickly teach your clients not to respect your time either. It is an attitude and belief that is transferred amazingly fast.

Just like any other of the previously mentioned business decisions, you get to choose. Are you a morning person willing to start seeing clients at 7am? Are you more of a night owl willing to work until 9 P.M.? Do you see kids primarily and have to adjust to their school schedules? When do you want to work? When are you at your best for your clients? When you can answer these questions, set your hours accordingly and stick to them.

That sounds almost too good to be true, and in some ways it is. That is "the perfect picture." Your real picture might be different right now. It doesn't have to be.

This is a conversation I've had with quite a few therapists. It goes something like this, "But my clients want to be seen at (insert time or hours that is different than your boundaries or when you want to work), what do I do?" This is what I know about this question and the answers I have been given from my own experience.

If you set your boundaries and stick to them, you are doing the right thing for yourself, and in doing that you role model healthy behavior, attitudes, and boundaries for your clients. Your behavior as equal an indicator of the kind of therapist you are as any words you can say. That message will be conveyed loud and clear to your clients and your community.

Clients who want to work with you will respect your boundaries, and, interestingly, those who could "only" see you at 9 P.M. on Friday will find a time that is consistent with your boundaries.

I know this because I've been there. I committed to myself and my family that I was not going to work on Fridays.

Ever.

After years of having to work until 11 P.M. or midnight on Fridays, I swore that those days were over. It was time for me to rededicate Friday night to my family. Of course, starting out in practice, I thought I had to conform to every client's wishes. It wasn't long before I started to schedule one or two clients on Fridays. That turned into a full day most Fridays, and then sometimes into Friday evening. It wasn't what I had planned. I was quickly going against my own boundaries.

The first indicator of a problem was my family being annoyed. Eventually leading to me being annoyed with myself and then my clients. My clients picked up that I was annoyed, and they showed their understanding by not showing up or canceling.

I was communicating loud and clear that I didn't respect my own boundaries, so why would they? Once I re-established those boundaries with myself and shared them with my clients, they got it. We scheduled for a time that was consistent with everyone's schedule and boundaries and got back to work. Your boundaries regarding your time, and your adherence to them or lack of respect for them, will communicate volumes to your clients.

Of course, this is also under the umbrella of "within the guidelines of the market forces." Just as we occasionally coach our clients to allow flexibility in their lives, we must, too. If you are planning on primarily seeing school-age children, I don't think it is fair to ask them to consistently miss school time each week to come to session. They have to be seen after school but not too late as to keep them up past a reasonable bed time. That requires flexibility on the part of the therapist.

There are some couples that struggle to have time for each other due to work schedules, meaning they only have one or two particular hours each week to come to counseling. That kind of situation might require our flexibility, at least initially. Let's face it, that is a problem facing MANY couples today, is often a source of discord, and therefore a clinical issue – but if you don't give them the chance to get in and get started, then we don't have the opportunity to help them change that.

So what is the bottom line? Have boundaries but be flexible in your hours and scheduling. Seems to contradict itself, doesn't it?

You can judge it by knowing yourself and in knowing what it means for you to be authentic clinically and professionally. If you feel annoyed with yourself for scheduling someone outside your boundaries, you are not being authentic. If you feel you were not flexible enough with the young couple who wanted to work with you, ditto. It's all about how you feel about yourself as a professional when setting boundaries. That is the message that comes through strongest to your clients.

If you are still questioning how to handle your hours and boundaries, I will give you an example of my schedule.

Monday, Tuesday, Wednesday: anything goes – I will start early and work late, if clients request. Usually, I will see couples and adult individuals during the day, and then school children and teens in the afternoon and evening. I will start as early as 8:30 A.M., but I usually start around a leisurely 11am. My last client is usually at 6 or 7 P.M., but I could go as late as 8 P.M. if needed once in a while. I will usually see five to six clients on each one of these days but might go as high as seven if I can spread them out through the day – I usually try to chunk clients in groups of two to three with an hour or two in between. M-T-W are pretty loose, but I know they are my "heavy" work days – heavy being I see the bulk of my clients in these three days.

Thursday is the day I will see the clients that couldn't make it earlier in the week. I try to schedule throughout the day but not into the evening. I try not to see clients past 5 P.M. on Thursday, especially if I have worked "late" all three nights before. Thursday is usually a nice family night. I start my weekend early Friday. I do my billing in the morning, maybe write a little throughout the day and do something in the evening with my family. Same thing for the weekends. I'll write a little over the weekend, but always make sure there is family time.

There are a few absolutes. I will never work so early that I cannot be home to wake my daughters up for school and have breakfast with them. I won't work more than three "late" (8 P.M.) nights in the week. I will always schedule around important events, field trips, school outings, or lunches with my family – as long as I know about them in advance. Every spring and fall, I slow down my practice and I trade in my late nights at the office to be a soccer coach for my girls.

These absolutes came about by NOT being able to do these things when I worked for somebody else. When my absolutes get "out-of-whack," I am not the person, professional, dad, husband, or friend I should be, so I work pretty hard not to let them get out-of-whack.

Those are my boundaries. What do yours look like? How do they need to be more firm? Where is there room for flexibility? What do you want your week to look like?

Documents & Policies

Rumor has it most therapists aren't very good at, or simply don't like "that paperwork stuff." But you've got to have it. At the very least there are a few documents you must have:

> **Financial agreement between you and your clients stating your fees and late cancellation policy.** You can't have firm boundaries as mentioned previously, if they are not spelled out and adhered to by both you and your clients.
>
> **General agreement of any rules or specific office policies.** This could be incorporated into the financial agreement, but I like to spell these out one more time. We have a policy against leaving children unattended in our waiting room – it's on the document. I also share the expectations for client sessions to be 45 to 50 minutes, unless previously agreed upon. It's important, again, for both you and your client to have these expectations firmly laid out before beginning work.
>
> **New client intake information** – the basic info you need to capture to form a client file. Depending on whether or not you use software, this may be laid out for you already. If not, it's fairly simple to create your own.
>
> **Initial assessment** – separate from the Intake form, this document asks more in-depth questions about why the client is choosing to enter in to therapy. It offers a helpful baseline and captures more information to start the process.
>
> **Release.** A general release of information has worked for me all these years. You can check with your local licensing body to find out what MUST be included in yours or consult with a peer.

These are the basics – you may need more depending on where you practice. I would encourage you to consult with your state and/or local licensing agency to make sure you have the required documents covered. I have found that they are more than happy to help.

If you have specific questions about these, I've included samples in the appendix in the back of the book. Take a look there for ideas. Most of these documents are going to look fairly similar where ever you practice, but each individual location might have individual specificities.

Insurance
Malpractice insurance is another "gotta have." You can find it through licensing and accrediting bodies for a pretty good cost. I think I spend around $320 each year for malpractice insurance – then I make sure I give the best client care possible in order to make sure that premium doesn't go up!

You have to have it, even if you never use it. Insurance companies will want to see it, as will CAQH and just about any other professional you work with. Plan for it, do the research, find a good premium, and buy it.

Website
In this day, it's a must. Start planning for it. For me, this is my primary marketing tool. It's the hub of sales and marketing for my practice. It is a necessary business item. I will talk more about it in the marketing section, but I wanted to get you thinking about it, if you haven't already, as a necessary part of your business. Whether it's static site with just your practice information or an updateable blog with additional resources, you will need a website to be successful in private practice.

Business cards
Another necessary business item that speaks volumes about you. Your website is an extension of your card, but your card is often the first thing prospective referral sources or clients will take with them once you are done chatting with them. It should leave a favorable impression.

Having said that, please don't opt for free business cards. Take the time and invest a small amount of money into making your card something memorable. There are plenty of options available that don't cost very much. I used MS Publisher to create my first card on my own and then invested less than $100 for 500 cards with multiple colors on quality paper from a professional printer:

Later, I invested in a logo from a pretty amazing artist – it was a few hundred dollars well spent that will go farther than just business cards. I took the logo and used the same program to design the card. This time I went with slightly better card stock and rounded edges for a little change – same printer, slightly different card.

Business Card 1   **Business Card 2**

I implore you, I beg you, take the time to create a solid business card or have one created for you. There are plenty of services out there that will do it for free, but the message you are sending to potential clients and referrals sources is much different than if you take the time and small investment it takes to create something that is uniquely yours.

Niche
Speaking of something that is uniquely yours… I want to take up just a little time discussing the idea of having a niche-practice. There are entire volumes written on the idea of creating a niche practice. I know quite a few coaches who focus extensively on the idea of niches practices. At one time, it was believed having a niche practice was "the only way" to go in to private practice. I believe it is helpful to work within a niche, but it isn't a must. You can have a niche, and still help other people who may not be in that niche, as long as you are qualified.

Just what is a niche practice? It is a practice that has a very well defined specialty and focus. This is more than just what your clinical credentials may define, it is the focus on working with a specific group in order to better define your market.

Developing a niche will help you to focus your sales and marketing information, your website, and your overall approach to your practice.
Examples of niche practice would be those therapists who specialize in working with pervasive developmental disorders, more specifically Asperger's disorder clients and their families, and those who work only with a particular age group using art or play therapy. You might find niche practices in the area

of working with couples who have experienced infidelity or a niche practice specializing in work with adolescent girls and eating disorders.

If you take the time to imagine your ideal client – those clients whom working with invigorates you and ignites your passion as a helping professional – you are your way to determining your niche. These are the clients you should be working with and focusing your efforts on during your working time. These should also be the clients you focus your marketing efforts on attracting.

It is helpful to consider your niche when working with a very specific kind of client or when marketing to a very specific client/referral source. This may be the area you are "most qualified" or "most passionate" about working with. I encourage you to consider YOUR niche as you move forward in to your practice.

As you define your niche, I think it's helpful and fun to determine what other areas are touched by this niche and what other areas you might be of service. For me, this came through my extensive work in the substance abuse field. At one time, my niche was ONLY substance-dependent adolescents. Over the years this has branched considerably into related areas – substance-dependent adolescents start as substance-abusing adolescents, who were once adolescents who experienced difficulty in life. Of course, struggling adolescents require help in getting their home life in order. This may often result in family sessions or parenting and marriage work with mom and dad. There have been times I found myself working with a substance-abusing adult parent because their substance-abusing child suggested they get help. Eventually working with adolescents lead to an interest in to how play therapy could help. Substance abuse and play therapy are certainly not in the same niche – but in my professional life they go hand in hand and allow me to work with a diverse array of clients.

I do not believe your niche has to be narrowly defined. I think your message does. You need to be able to explain what you do to potential referral sources much more succinctly than what I just did.

However, I don't think your practice has to be that narrow. It should be within your area of expertise. But shouldn't your expertise be diverse but related? It's an interesting conversation that surrounds niche versus generalist today. It's both philosophical and practical. I encourage you to define your practice as you see fit; but most importantly, you will need to define your message – we'll talk about more in Marketing.

Client model
Personal growth versus medical model – this is an interesting concept I've always felt at an intuitive level in my "therapist gut".

Working in community health centers, agencies, and in the insurance field certainly sets us up as helping professionals to approach our clients from a medical model of treatment – that is the DIAGNOSIS, TREATMENT PLAN, 12 SESSION-OR-LESS SOLUTION. That is what insurance companies pay for, and what many agencies measure success by.

This is a great model when you are treating depression or anxiety exclusively. There is considerable research that highlights the best short-term methods to treating these diagnoses.

> Developing a niche will help you to focus your sales and marketing information, your website, and your overall approach to your practice.

HOWEVER, you will find that you are not treating these diagnoses exclusively.
You and I both know that depression and anxiety often come with co-occurring co-morbidities, if you want to use the DSM/medical terminology. Below the current depressive episode may be years of low self-esteem brought on by a negligent mother who passed away and was never grieved for. Are you going to treat the depression in six sessions and then discharge the client as the medical model would prescribe, or should you address the underlying concerns related to the individuals stunted personal growth?

I like to think of it as "people are people," and they come to our office with a variety of situations that they could benefit from our time, attention, and insight. Human behavior comes with a myriad of variables that are sometimes outside the brief treatment plans of the medical model.

Very rarely, if ever, have I worked with a client who has presented with ONLY depression, and not had any further concerns that benefitted from therapeutic work.

It is important to work with the WHOLE person and not just the diagnosis. To understand the client's history and what may have triggered his depression or anxiety and then work to understand the possibility of future triggers and help the client avoid future occurrences WHILE helping the client understand themselves and their goals for their life is just the cusp of working with the "whole person."

This is more the idea of a *"personal growth"* understanding of treatment than working from the strict medical model. This is the core concept inherent in private practice; the ability to work with and help the whole person. However, it is not a model most insurance companies like or will support.

Therefore, it is important to come to an understanding with yourself, and how you will approach working with your clients, so that you can explain that to them from the start, and remind them of that when the insurance company stops authorizing treatment after 12 sessions. Your clients will appreciate your candid description of your believes about treatment, will respect you for it, and may decide to continue work after insurance stops paying.

More importantly, I think it is the "right" thing to do – to work to help the whole person, not just solve the problem of the diagnosis. In doing that, we respect our clients as human beings and not the label we are asked to apply to them.

In a business sense, this is doing good business, as it builds up your positive reputation in your community and helps you define your goal as a clinician. Adopting this mindset will also let clients know that you are available to help them whenever they have a difficult time in life, not just when their concerns meet the diagnostic criteria.

Relations with your former employer – When it is time to leave
This is an experience that is chock full of variables for everyone – it really all depends on where you work, who your supervisor is, and what past experiences have been.

The variables:

Timing – how much time is the right time to give notice?
For your clients, I would like to say at least 30 to 60 days, especially if you will be transitioning to a far-away location where they will not be able to continue treatment with you. This seems to be the ethical amount of time to give them to help wrap up treatment, if appropriate, and deal with any issues related to loss or abandonment.

On the other hand, your clients may decide they want to continue working with you and will make the transition with you. For your practice, this is wonderful, as it will help you start your practice with a partial caseload!
But, what is good for your business may be interpreted as "not so good" for the agency you may be leaving. It is important to proceed with caution and have a good feel for how you think your agency may respond.

I have heard of different employers releasing therapists on the spot when they submit their notice, and I have worked with therapists who have been granted the appropriate time necessary to do an effective job closing out their cases, transferring their clients, and moving on. For me personal, most experiences I have had have been rather bittersweet – sweet for me, unfortunately bitter from my employer.

These are the important things to remember:

Your client has the right make an informed decision about where and from whom they wish to receive treatment.

You have the right to choose where you want to work and should not feel bullied in to staying anywhere you don't want to be.

In working with therapists transitioning into private practice, it is always my goal to help them leave their previous employment in a positive and professional manner.

"Professional manner" relates to several points:

- Giving your employer enough notice of your transition, generally 14-30 days notice
- Informing your clients of your move well in advance; generally 30 days prior

Completing any remaining paperwork, notes, treatment plans

Fortunately, we get to choose our own behavior and attitude as we go through this process. Unfortunately, there are those who may choose to act differently then we do. That it was why I encourage caution in making the decision as to how and when you will notify your employer. Some will be supportive, some will not – be prepared to deal with both.

There is one more critical variable to factor in; your personal feelings about what I call, "Living the Double-Life." This is that transition time in the middle of deciding you are going to open your practice, the time you are putting everything in place to when you leave your employer to be in your practice.

For me, and for many of the therapists I have coached, this is a time of greatest insecurity and feeling overwhelmed. There is the tendency to feel like you are not being completely honest with your employer – and in a way you are not – as you start to move towards your private practice and away from their employment. This is often the time many therapists stop moving forward and allow themselves to be stuck.

Stuck by fear, stuck by insecurity, stuck by loyalty to their employer and not to themselves; there are quite a few ways to feel stuck.

That is why I encourage you NOT to prolong this period. The quicker you act on your decision and move forward, the less time you have to live your professional life through cognitive dissonance. The less chance you have of getting stuck, or even worse, deciding not to act on your dream.

This is THE time to have a network of like-minded peers or a mentor/coach. The accountability that can be provided during this time from a group or coach is far more than we can often provide for ourselves. Know that there are plenty of people willing to help you and many of us who have made the jump to private practice – you CAN do it!

If you are reading this book, and you can put these ideas into practice, I believe you can be in a successful and authentic private practice within the next 12 months. I once thought of this as my "five-year plan" when I worked for somebody else. When I finally got motivated, it took 11 months. I've seen others do it quicker.

The Private Practice Field Manual
Nuts and Bolts Checklist

Development your business mindset
- $$$ Money
- ⌛Time
- ☺Team and resources

Location, location, location.
- 📍Where are you going to practice?

Office – what does it look like?
- ☐ Therapy room
- ☐ Waiting area
- ☐ Lobby
- ☐ Restroom

Business Name
{*What will people say?*}

Professional Licenses
- ☐ Are they all in order?

To accept insurance or not to accept insurance –*THAT is the question*
- ☐ Yes or No, or are you an Insurance Eclectic
- ☐ CAQH
- ☐ NPI
- ☐ Shop for Insurance Companies

Finances
- ☐ How will you track?
- ☐ Who will you consult with for tax purposes?

What's your Salary
- $$$How much do you want to earn? Do the math!

The Private Practice Field Manual
Nuts and Bolts Checklist (cont'd)

Billing
- How will you get paid? Someone else or do-it yourself? Who or what?

Hours
- When will you work?

Documents and Policies
- Create your own, but check out mine in the Appendix

Professional Liability Insurance
- Get some

Website
- Start thinking about it, because it's a BIG part of the marketing section!

Business Cards
NO FREEBIES!

Niche
- What's your specialty?
- Who's your ideal client?
- Who else are you really good at helping?

Client model
- Medical Model *or* Personal Growth

When is it time to go
1. Map out your strategy
2. Put it on the calendar
3. Execute

4

MARKETING Your Practice

Marketing. This a concept we are not so prepared for in grad school.

The belief we are taught is that there are professionals in the agencies we will work for who will take care of all of that – we don't have to worry. That's about the extent of the education we get on it.

Many of us may have a bad taste in our mouths when it comes to these ideas. "Sales" drums up ugly pictures of used car salesmen with slicked-back hair and pencil-thin mustaches in checker-patterned sport coats, chewing on a 3-day old toothpick not letting you leave the car lot after you've been there for half the day.

"Marketing" reminds us of all the slick "Snake Oil 2.0" being peddled out there in disingenuous ways with words like "NEW and IMPROVED," "WHAT'S OLD IS NEW," and "GENUINELY AUTHENTIC."

It doesn't have to be that way for you.

Marketing – the business term, can be fun and enjoyable when it comes to your practice. It is more like Connecting and Community Building, or Relationship Building and Sharing Your Knowledge. The bottom line, Sales and

Marketing is one more way you can reach out and help people, if done correctly, and in a way that is consistent with your beliefs and values as a helping professional.

Clients will come to you in primarily two distinctly different but related ways, they are referred directly to you from referral sources you have cultivated or they find you from some manner of advertising. Occasionally these methods are interwoven, that is usually a sign that you have created a "the perfect system" for your practice, and it is working on all cylinders.

Although there are two primary ways in which clients come to work with you – by referral and by advertising; there is an absolute smorgasbord of opportunity as to how to engage in these activities.

Advertising tends to be the easiest way, but also the most expensive and usually least effective. Advertising consists of creating some form of interruption that is paid for in order to get your name and information in front of potential clients or partners in an attempt to convince them to engage in a desired behavior – usually a purchasing / buying behavior. It is generally thought that the "best" interruption will get the most attention, and therefore get the most business. Unfortunately, the concept of "best" interruption is continually researched and continually changes. There are research and marketing firms who make billions in determining how to "best" interrupt portions of your day to get their product's message in front of you.

Examples of advertising:

Billboards	PHONE BOOK ADDS	US Post mail campaigns
TV COMMERCIALS	Radio commercials	BROCHURE DROP OFF
Info-mercials	RADIO JINGLES	Pay-per click ads
FACEBOOK ADS	Google Adwords	PRODUCT PLACEMENT
Magazine Ads	NEWSPAPER ADS	Celebrity Endorsement
PRESS RELEASES	Email Campaigns	SPAM ADVERTISING
Banner Ads	FIND-A-THERAPIST SITES	

I am sure there are more examples – each one with it's own unique subset of advertising opportunities.

Advertising is usually very broad-based. It's an attempt to get the message out in the biggest way possible, to the most people, in order to increase the percentage of those who respond. This works fairly well with large scale, consumable products – soda pop for example. The company who gets their product in your face the most, in the most appealing way, wins. Usually, this is directly related to cost, as trying to do the "most" in advertising is closely related to paying the "most" – see Super Bowl commercials as a prime example. This doesn't always work in the mental health field. Our "customers" are more specific in what they are looking for. They are not looking for soda, they are looking for relief. Therefore, the advertising, if you choose to use it, needs to be more specialized. You are looking for a few very specific individuals, depending on your specialty. You don't need to bring in the caseload of a large community mental health agency with a large operating budget, do you? Generally speaking, most private practitioners operate well with a weekly caseload of 20 to 30 clients. Knowing this, how would these numbers effect your spending on advertising?

ADVERTISING FAILURES

Before I talk about what works, let me go ahead and share my advertising failures with you. These are is my experience – are they meant to deter you? Yeah, somewhat.

These are ventures I went in thinking, in my gut, that it probably wasn't a good idea, but I did it anyway. I went against sage advice and my own instinct because the allure of advertising can be that great.

Was it self-fulfilling prophecy? Somewhat. These were all the ideas I had read about and had been told "won't work". However, these ideas just appeared "too easy to fail." I thought "it has to succeed, because it is so easy –those others just didn't do it right". I had that attitude that if I did the easy advertising, just a little better than those that said it didn't work, it would work for me. Even after reading this, you might decide to give it a try, and I wish you the best of luck – it IS easy. Hopefully, you succeed if you try them. However, if you fail, learn from the failure, that is what the failure is for. I just want to encourage you one more time, there are BETTER ways to fail, DO NOT try these…

Let's talk BIG failures first.

United States Postal Mail Brochure Campaign

When I first got started in practice, I went with the easiest of easy assignments, despite reading and hearing from several sources that it just wasn't going to work. Well, I thought, "I'm going to do it differently; I'm going to do it better". Rather than sending out brochures telling professionals in the community that I was open for business, my idea was to send out brochures advertising a training of one of my unique niche areas – assessing and treating substance abuse in teens.

I designed a rather nice brochure in Windows Publisher, invested in a new printer and several color ink cartridges so that could print them at home for about $50, combed through several phone books to build my list of 200, bought $88 worth of stamps, wrestled with the home printer to print 200 appropriate looking copies of the brochure, addressed them and sent them out the door. It was a pretty difficult and time consuming process, even though it sounds easy. It took 'only' about $150, but quite a bit of time.

My response rate: 0.5 percent - one person – and she was a colleague I had been chatting with as we both were working on building our practices, so does that really count?

I would call that a pretty abysmal failure.

But, as with all failures – lessons learned.

> **If you are going to print in bulk (anything over five) go with a professional printer.** They are a bargain when you consider the time, energy, frustration, and money wasted trying to print at home AND the product is considerably better – that's why THEY are the professional printer and I am the therapist.
>
> **Brochures don't work as effectively as we would like**, especially in our time of hyper-connectivity, people usually don't even open "junk mail." I don't, even if the brochure IS really well designed… Don't waste your time or theirs giving them more junk mail.

Open House

I tell you, I REALLY wanted this one to work. I was going in on the opportunity with my two office partners: two wonderful women who have quite a bit more history in the community than I do. Since they were the seasoned professionals, I thought that there would just be a huge turnout. I thought it would be an epic success.

There wasn't a huge turnout. It was pretty frustrating. But the crab dip was good.

There was a lot of work put into it too; far more than my own little brochure campaign. We essentially did the brochure campaign to let people know we were having the open house, and then had to do all the food and drink preparation ($), office / site preparation (*time, lots of time*), and door prize purchasing ($). We also offered "discount cards," cards referral sources could give to potential clients for a discounted initial session ($ *and time*). After it was all said and done, a summer's worth of planning and about $1000 split between the three of us, the results were less than we had hoped for.

I'm fairly certain we mailed out around 400 invitations. We had less than 20 people show up through the four-hour period, less than a 5 percent response rate. It's going to take a lot of crab dip to convince me to do that again.

Lessons learned:

People, even those you work closely with to help the community, don't always want to interrupt their day to come visit, even if there is good food available. Most people don't like their day being interrupted to open junk mail, they're not going to interrupt their day for bigger interruptions, no matter how great the opportunity. For more on interruption versus permission marketing, I highly recommend you check out the works of Seth Godin.

Throwing more and more money at an advertising venture does not guarantee its success. We put quite a lot of money and time into this, but it still didn't matter. We were asking people to interrupt their day, and they were not prepared to do that.

Door-to-door/office-to-office "is the doctor in" stops

This plan – this was "The One" – this was the idea that was going to fill my practice in no time. Since I had the extra time early in my practice, when I was only seeing 10 to 12 clients each week, I thought I could dedicate that extra time to driving around the local communities to get in front of the primary care physicians. I figured they weren't going to have time to open and flip through my brochures, but certainly they would have time to stop what they were doing and chat with me for a few minutes – I mean, it was "Me" that would be coming to their office – why wouldn't they stop to chat, right? They couldn't stop to chat because physicians are busy, busy people – so are their receptionists and nurse practitioners. They work in a very busy environment, surrounded by busy people who are busy being ill. Most doctors complain that they do not have enough time to truly focus on their patients, much less any other anomaly that introduces itself into their day, like me.

They didn't have time to chat with me.

I left my information and a few business cards with whomever was the least busy at that moment. Usually it took 20 to 30 minutes to find someone who wasn't busy simply to take my card and maybe get it to the doctor.

Response rate = 0 percent.

Lesson learned:
> Doctors offices are busy places that don't always have time and certainly don't always appreciate you just dropping in to talk about how "not busy" you are. There are better ways to get physicians attention.

> I learned this a few years later, from a friend who had made a career of marketing and selling to physicians – he sold everything from prescription medications to lasers and prescription counting computers. His lesson – "It takes quite a bit of time to get in front of a doctor – they have HUNDREDS of people stopping by their offices every week." It appears my idea wasn't so unique.

Advertising that works
So what works when it comes to advertising? Where should you focus your advertising dollars?

These are the advertising endeavors that have worked for me, as well as for some of therapists I have worked with or collaborated with.

Phone books
Not the most creative first answer. But it is first because it is the advertising area that can be the simplest. However, it is still one that requires the most thought and consideration. It used to be pretty simple to place an ad in a

phone book. You selected your package from one of four or five different options, crafted your ad, and then let it rip – paying every month or for a full year of advertising. Phone books used to be the primary source of information for people looking for businesses that they didn't know much about. Usually, in the past, the most well-crafted phone book ad won and brought in the most business.

That's not the case anymore.

Phone books are no longer the primary source for information. Obviously, since you were able to find THIS book online, you probably already know this. As you have noticed, the internet and all its many facets are where most people go to find a particular business. They are able find out quite a bit more about the business, its owner, and its employees than just a phone number and address, but we will talk more about that later.

There is a very specific client who will use the phone book over the internet to find you. They either already know you and your name and just want a quick reference for your phone number, or they are not technology savvy internet users. Both of these sets of clients are becoming more and more rare, as it is likely quicker to find your name, number, and address from a cell phone or smartphone. the idea of individuals NOT using the internet is fading, although there are people out there who don't. These two factors and client profiles should be considered when you think about how much money you want to spend on phone book print advertising to attract those clients.

Phone books got wise to these facts in the past few years as there revenue started to plummet. They have started to offer a variety of internet advertising packages as well. This is where your careful consideration and attention is needed. I am not sure the internet packages are always as valuable as we may think; they might be, but my experiences have suggested differently.

Here are three reasons/case studies why:

I was offered a "**Grrrrreat Opportunity**" by one of our local phone books, a national outfit or at least they had part of a national outfit name in their name. They did not produce a standard paper phone book but offered a DVD/CD ROM that they dispersed to a large section of the country. They promised me the world, the sky, and everything in between – AND I was going to be included in a DVD/CD ROM, that meant I was using "new technology"! Being fairly new to the game, I jumped on this "Grrrrreat Opportunity" – I mean it was "guaranteed" to fill my practice!

I probably should have done a little bit more research before jumping on this Grrrrreat Opportunity.

It didn't work. Apparently, this disk was published and send out in another part of the country, which would have been Grrrrreat if I was selling products across state lines, or online, but my business at the the time required clients to be present in my office. Unfortunately, there was a rather large bill I am still paying on bit by bit. So far, I have not received a single client from this advertising venture, and it has been very expensive. You really have to research what you are buying when it comes to internet phone book advertising
The next opportunity was from another local phone book (yeah, I can't believe we have this many local phone books either). Their internet package, for only an extra $30 (deleted "dollars") per month, guaranteed I would be on Google and "at the top of the Google searches for your area."

I was already on Google – I put myself there. You can do that, too, for A LOT cheaper than $30 per month! I think the rate to put yourself on Google is around FREE. You can even put a handy little map and a bit of information about yourself too. You can do that for Yahoo Search as well. Without the phone book company. Having already known that, I didn't bite on this offer, and you shouldn't either. Do the legwork of putting yourself in these search engines, put the information you want there, and then work on your SEO – search engine optimization – with someone who knows about it. You don't have to pay phone book companies to put you on the internet. Do it yourself and save $360+ per year.

My final phone book story relates to a newer idea – using mobile devices to find therapists. This particular advertising package offered to ensure that I was at "the top of the list" for anyone who used this particular outfit's mobile device application to search for therapy. Of course, this particular company was guaranteeing that their application was automatically included in every new mobile phone and smartphone being sold in the US... Except mine. Strangely, I had just purchased a new smartphone, and that app was not on my phone.

But I bit at the opportunity anyway – at a cost of $41 per month for a one-year contract. When I called after two months to report that I had not received ANY business from the purchase of this product, I was kindly informed that I had received several hundred "hits" – people finding my name – but they had not translated over to business. I was also informed that "No, we will not cancel your contract until the end of the year." They did kindly take my response to "automatically" cancel my contract as soon as it was up. So far, I have received several thousand hits, none of which have translated to business. Quite honestly, I am still not sure what this advertising product is doing for me, other than costing me over $480 for the year...

Now, despite these failures, I am still an advocate for phone book advertising. It definitely has its place. There are still people who use the phone book, and you need to be in there. Do you have to buy a full page ad? Should you invest in the "Gold Package" internet ad? I don't know. They didn't work for me. But you have to make your decision on where that advertising dollar goes. For me, I have cut back on my phone book advertising budget. I have the simplest of ads in each one of the "major" phone books in the area, and I have said "no thanks" to the "new" phone books trying to start up in the area. I want potential clients directed to my website through these ads, so that they get more information about me, my work, and who I am. From there, we can discuss whether or not I am a good fit for them either over the phone, or via email.

My original phone book adventures did help to fill my practice in the beginning, but it was a very "hit or miss" approach. I think it was important to be in the phone books initially, but now that my practice is full and thriving, and I have a system to keep it going, I don't need to rely on the phone books. I am still in them, for those who wish to find me there, but it is not a big component of my marketing strategy or my marketing budget.

My advice to you is to use caution when deciding on your advertising contracts – especially when it comes to the phone book. You are signing up for a year-long contract that they will not easily break if you are unhappy with the results after only a few months.

It may be necessary to get in to all the local phone books when you are just starting out, but be thoughtful and strategic about how you spend those phone book advertising dollars. If there are a lot of providers already listed in the books, you may want to find a way to stand out – it might help to pay for a premium package for the first year of your practice. If you are one of only a few providers in the phonebooks, then frugality is likely to be your best bet. Either way, the phone book tends to be a random generator of referrals, like most advertising is. There are quite a few variables to whether or not potential clients call you, not all of which are within your control. It is helpful to be in the phone books, but it shouldn't be your only strategy.

Connecting with a therapy locator system
This has been the best use of my advertising dollar thus far, and I have heard similar results from other helping professionals as well.

There are quite a few therapist locator services available. Many states have their own local therapist locator databases, as do different licensing agencies, certification bodies, and insurance companies. I know I can be found on our state website for my licenses as well as in the play-therapist directory on the Association for Play Therapy website (www.A4PT.com) and then with any insurance company I am in-network with.

These services are usually free for members. As I think about it though, membership is rarely free. Consider the cost as part of your dues or license renewal fee.

But professional therapy locator services are a bit different. These are paid advertising where you enter in your information, usually quite a bit more than with a phone book ad, and the locator service does quite a bit of work with search engines and their own advertising to make sure you are found. In a way, I see it as pooling your advertising dollar with other therapists to get more bang for your buck. The work that these services put in to search engine optimization and their own advertising to insure that you are found is usually top notch. You can't get that kind of exposure on your own.

You can find out more about some of the sites like MyTherapistMatch.com, GoodTherapy.com, FindCounseling.com, or PsychologyToday.com simply by looking them up on the internet. Most offer a free sample of their services for a month.

I have enjoyed the services of Psychology Today for the past several years. For about $30 per month, I am listed in their search engines. I usually receive three to five calls or emails from their service each month, so the service really pays for itself fairly quickly.

I would note that I was rather fortunate; I was one of the only therapists within a 20 to 30 mile radius to begin using Psychology Today. THAT factor was fairly helpful in clients choosing to call me first. If you are about to be the hundredth therapist in a five-block radius joining a site, your dollars may be better spent elsewhere, unless you work to separate yourself (there's that niche idea again) from the rest of the pack.

Interestingly, I have worked with a quite a few therapists recently who have reported outstanding results with Psychology Today, even in quite large metro areas. In the same breath, they have shared that the helping professional down the hall may receive zero referrals, while they are bringing them in daily from their therapist locator work. This points to two factors: (1) again, the apparent randomness of advertising and the myriad of variables that go in to whether or not a potential client selects you over the person farther up or down on the page; (2) the importance of constructing your profile in a professional and appealing manner that speaks to your ideal client.
It is important to consider the information that you place on these locator sites. You have to have enough, but not too much. It's got to be written correctly, but not "APA style" correctly. I will get into that more when we discuss websites and the internet.

I do encourage you to try out at least one therapy locator service. The one I have used has been very good to me. As always, carefully consider the variables before spending your advertising dollar. Is it a long-term contract (mine I can end at any time), will people who want to find you be likely to use that site or find it through the sites advertising, are there additional perks to working with that site (I get a free subscription to Psychology Today by using the service – great read, and great waiting room material).

Writing as advertising
Documenting a string of brilliant, insightful, and helpful ideas, attaching your name to it, and putting it out in the world is easier than it ever has been. Writing, publishing, and establishing yourself as an expert in your area of specialization is an inexpensive way to build your credibility and attract potential clients.

There are a variety of ways to do this, with a variety of services and websites that will support your goals. I have used Constant Contact, 1Shopping Cart, Wordpress, and EzineArticles.com over the years, and I have heard good things about Mad Mimi, Google blogs, and Yahoo blogs. Some of the services are free, some may cost between $15-30 per month. Do some searching online to find out what service is best for you. Each one of these offers a slight variation on the idea, but they all have the same general goal – to take your writing and disperse in a manner that is helpful in building your credibility and your business.

The process is fairly simple. As helping professionals, I know you have a ton of great ideas, techniques, and suggestions the world needs to hear about – ways to cope with stress, relaxation techniques, suggestions for family building, couples exercises – the list could go on. You have great ideas to share that can help people, so share them.

Decide how often you want to write. I've known some therapists to write once a day, and others who write once a month. Me, I send out an article each week at 8:55 A.M. EST Monday morning to clients, potential clients, friends, and people who have requested to receive the article. From there, I post the article on my website, share it on Facebook, Tweet about it, and then send it to EzineArticles.com. If you've got something to share, why limit it to just one outlet, right?

Using one of the systems I mentioned before, I can write the article any time I want or write several and save them up for later distribution, put them into the system, and set it up to be sent whenever I want. Depending on what system you use, you can set up a very nice, professional looking newsletter template, put your article in and hit send. The article goes out to your list of people. You get to share your wisdom and insight, and your client and potential clients are delighted to receive just a little bit of extra help to get them through the week. Ideally, they find you so brilliant that they share your ideas with other people, and the legend of your brilliance spreads.

How do you find these people to send your brilliance to? How do you build your list?

There are quite a few ways. First, add your current clients. Of course, ask their permission (it's illegal not to have their permission), and then you can go into whatever system you use and enter their email address. Same for potential clients, you can ask them during your initial conversation if they would like to receive information from you, add them to the list, and this will provide a touch point for them to learn more about you.

The best, and my favorite, way to build your list is through having a sign-up button on your website. (Have you noticed how all things tend to point to your website?) Every one of the systems I mentioned has a way to put a simple sign-up box on your website. If you find a system that doesn't have this ability you can easily find a "web-person" to quickly get you set up.

This is an awesome way to build a list of current and potential clients. People find you on line through your website, they like what they see, but they want to know more. You can offer a "free sample" of your work – a tip sheet, or a relaxation technique – something you think potential clients will benefit from. Ask them to enter their email address so that you can send them the tip sheet – most services have an "autoresponder" that you can set up to do that for you. They sign up, they get the sheet, and you get an opportunity to offer them continued support and insight until they are ready to enter into a therapeutic alliance. It really is a great system for building your credibility and letting people know about your expertise. Any one of the systems I mentioned will walk your right through the entire process – getting it all set up takes just a few hours, or of course, you could contract out with a web-design group.

I really feel like putting fresh and insightful information out is a necessity in today's practice-building environment. It is an opportunity for inexpensive, permission-based advertising for you. But more importantly, it is an opportunity for your community to learn about you, about what you have to offer, and to gain helpful information. It is truly a win-win situation.

Now, if you are going to write, why not write on a larger scale? The email list/article blog is a great opportunity to build credibility and help your local community, there are also larger scale opportunities for this as well. It is an opportunity for you to help more people, more often, on a larger scale.

I have really enjoyed the benefits of writing for different idea warehouses and distributors. EzineArticles.com is a common one a lot of people use. It is a simple website where you sign up to be an author, submit your articles, and allow them to be distributed to anyone searching for your particular ideas.

Most often, the people who are searching this site are more of a professional nature – producers or editors looking for authors and idea creators. I have been granted several speaking engagements and radio opportunities simply through putting my articles on EzineArticles.com. There are quite a few more opportunities out there on the internet – Ehow.com, About.com, ChaCha.com, InfoBarrel.com – more than I can list here. If you are going to write for clients and potential clients, why not let the rest of the world know of your brilliance as well?

Writing doesn't just have to be internet based either. You can offer your work to local newspapers, submit to magazines, or write for trade journals. The important part is that you are contributing to your community of potential clients and building your reputation as an expert in your field – and you ARE an expert! The world needs to know you – and writing is one of the best and easiest ways to let the world know.

> Let me just get right to it – relationship building ALWAYS works. If it doesn't work, then you are not doing it; you are doing something else.

I know I promised this section was going to be about advertising – marketing in its paid form – but did you notice how quickly "marketing and advertising" translated into "building expertise and sharing it with the world"? That is the BEAUTY of what we do! It doesn't have to be all "gross and icky" used car salesman lingo. It truly is about sharing your knowledge and wisdom with those who need it! Marketing for the helping professional is about sharing – not crafting the most expensive and attention-grabbing (interrupting) billboard, but about SHARING YOUR WISDOM, INSIGHT, KNOWLEDGE, AND EXPERTISE with the world! How cool is that?!

Marketing Reframed
Relationship building that works

Let me just get right to it – relationship building ALWAYS works. If it doesn't work, then you are not doing it; you are doing something else.

Relationship building – just the nature of the idea means you are building connections, helping your community, and sharing your expertise. By engaging in this activity, you are marketing and selling your practice in the most authentic way possible for helping professionals.

The difference with advertising and relationship building is, essentially, cost. Relationship building will cost you time, and possibly money, to go out and engage your community. It will take more effort and preparation than advertising, it will take a greater investment of your time and money resources, but the returns are greater. In building strategic relationships with referral partners, community leaders, and your community in general, you will be "putting yourself out there," rather than putting your dollar out there. You can do this from your office using the internet or by going out into the world and sharing yourself. Either way works, sometimes which works best may depend on your particular community as well as your preferences and personality.

Here are some of the activities you can do to starting building relationships in your community.

Public speaking (teaching, networking groups) BNI, Toastmasters, Rotary Club, chamber of commerce), social networking and "meet-ups"

Public speaking can come in many forms, each of which with its own variables, each one possessing a great opportunity for positive returns to you and your business. You can teach at a local college or university, participate in networking groups like Business Networking International (BNI), Rotary clubs, chambers of commerce, or seek out social networking meet-ups. There are a ton of opportunities in both large communities and small.

However, this tends to be one of those ideas that often sends therapists' pulse racing, blood pressure sky-rocketing, and knees shaking. Especially for those of us who are of a more introverted style.

I would have rather gone through a root canal with no anesthetic than hop up in front of a group of people and talk. My first speech class in high school was an abysmal failure and is still burned into my psyche after all these years. I think the teacher allowed me to pass the class out of fear I might die if I had to repeat it. My first (and I think only) speech in that class was red-faced, sweat-dripping, heart-pounding disaster that had my teacher wondering if she should call an ambulance.

I still feel that way before every speech I give.
But it gets better.

I was fortunate (I can say that now) to be put into a position early on in my professional career where I had to speak to a group of 60 or more people at least once, usually twice each week. At first it was a set speech I had to give, then it went into riffing about things I knew – sometimes things I wasn't always sure about. I had to get over that fear eventually. Small amounts of success in the endeavor and a few minor personal victories helped keep that going.

From there, I made the mistake of agreeing to do more. Eventually I was selected to talk to newspaper reporters, then local TV reporters, then national TV reporters, eventually larger groups of people. It was a wickedly slow and insidious path to force me to become comfortable with my own voice and sharing it with other people. It worked. Eventually it became a little easier. Practice, even "live practice" before cameras or high school auditoriums full of people became fairly easy. I still felt anxious before each situation, but I was able to push through it to get to the success on the other side.

Today, I force myself to maintain control over that anxiety by purposely throwing myself into these kinds of endeavors. I teach - there's nothing to induce anxiety like walking into a classroom of general psychology students, only 50 percent of whom WANT to be there, the other 50 percent who HAVE to be there. I quickly learned to keep my breakfast down, slow my racing heart, and stop stuttering in order to be able to speak coherently, eventually I was able to actually teach, now I might even try to joke.

I have also forced myself to volunteer to speak in front of our church once every few weeks. Usually, when I know my turn is coming up, I doubt myself for four or five days, curse myself for volunteering, and then attempt to rationalize ways out of it. Once it is over, I feel pretty groovy about having done it.

The point I am trying to make in sharing these examples is this:
NOBODY "enjoys" PUBLIC SPEAKING

But we learn to tolerate it; we can even become good at it. Once you accomplish those two things, tolerance and effectiveness, the personal and professional benefits far outweigh the desire to scream and run away from your audience.

The important part, at least for me, starting out, was to have some guidance, maybe even a script in some instances. Teaching comes from a curriculum and a text. There is guidance and ideas to share, you then get to mix in some of your own experience. The same is true for speaking at church. It's actually more of reading. It's already there for me; I just get to add my unique inflection.

These ideas go well with any speaking opportunity. If you take some time to prepare, and speak about things you are knowledgeable and comfortable with, YOU WILL BE SUCCESSFUL. You might feel terrible leading up to it, during it, and even a little bit after, but it will be worth it. There are many groups, books, and professionals out there to help you get comfortable with public speaking. But whatever you do, I really must encourage you to get comfortable with it and give it a try. Not only is it a great opportunity to build relationships, but, again, the world needs it. We need to hear your individual and unique brilliance.

In time, you may even want to come up with your own unique speaking topic or speech. I know quite a few therapists who have been very successful and well respected for giving speeches on the same topic to different groups. They have become known and are requested for their speech. What a great opportunity to share and build your credibility!

Of course, with your unique knowledge, wisdom, and experience as a helping professional, I am sure you could speak well on quite a few topics. Find the places in your community that need to hear that message and share with them!

You can find a multitude of opportunities depending on where you practice – whether it is a big city, small town, or anywhere in between, there are people who want to hear your message. It may be a group of 10, or a lecture hall of 100s; maybe even conferences of 1,000s. I think once you get started, and get comfortable, the opportunities are endless. Some of the places that have worked for me or therapists I have worked with:

Mental Health Groups

I know of several groups of people who meet a few times a month to discuss their own mental health, or that of their family members, and they are always looking for helpful advice and coping strategies. One of my favorite speeches for groups like this has been to offer a top-10 list of coping strategies or healthy habits. From that simple list, we get a great conversation going and the speech is a hit.

These are great groups to work with and they are usually happy to have you speak at and share your knowledge. You can find them in your community usually by doing an internet search for support groups in your specialty area.

Parent Nights at Schools
What a great chance for therapists who specialize in play therapy or working with families! Not always easy to get in to, but working with the school counselor or guidance department starts the relationship, and gives you a chance to get in front of parents.

Libraries
Local public libraries do a great job advertising speakers and presentations, and typically charge very little to rent the space to speak. They may often allow you to speak for free as long as you are not charging people to attend. This is a great place to practice public speaking, and to work on sharing your knowledge with your local community.

Church Groups
Local church groups often ask for experts in our field to share with their congregation. Another great chance to build credibility, and get your message of helping out into the community.

These are just a few ideas. There are plenty more opportunities – at first you may need to ask around to see who might want or need a speaker, but as you reputation grows, the opportunities will come looking for you.

Local Business Networking Organizations
Another opportunity for your relationship building and budding public speaking skill would be to attend or even join one of the local business networking organizations. Business Networking International (BNI), Rotary clubs, chambers of commerce, and other local networking opportunities exist in most communities in a fairly quiet way, unless you become a part of them. They are great places to build relationships with other professionals in your

community, and to work on various referral partnerships.
You can find BNI online and search for a group near you, you'd be amazed at how many people you find there. Check them out at BNI.com. I also recommend checking in to the more local business networking opportunities. Each group is different from location to location, so you will have to assess which ones are best suited for your needs. Whatever you do, research some of the local groups and start to work on a general network through these different opportunities.

Social Media
Social media is the "next greatest thing" when it comes to building professional relationships. By no means am I an "expert" in the realm of social media, but I have made it work pretty well for me and my practice, and I've worked with some pretty smart people in the emerging field of social media. Let me tell you what I have done.

First, I use LinkedIn (www.linkedin.com) to build professional relationships. This is a focused and very professional realm to connect with people you know professionally. You can also connect with people you have worked with or are currently working with. The key component to LinkedIn is its professional nature. This site is all about work relationships and professional exchanges. Use it to build connections in your local community, as well as in your professional community.

This is a great tool to mitigate the "lonely island" phenomenon that is common in individual private practice. LinkedIn makes it very easy to reach out and collaborate with a variety of professionals locally, nationally, and internationally.

Go to their website and sign up for a free account. From there you can connect with past peers from grad school or other work experiences. I've found it helpful to join some of the discussion groups there as well. There are quite a few groups with outstanding discussion topics. You can feel free to look me up as well.

I use Twitter quite a bit to connect as well. It is fairly simple to get started with a Twitter account (find me @Think_Change) and "follow" people or organizations of interest to you. I use the website to learn about what other therapists and helping professionals are up to, as many of us share our writings on Twitter. It's a great place to quickly share ideas and find new ones. You can also connect with peers throughout the world. I follow leaders and Tweeters in other areas of interest as well – sports, camping, social media, etc. I encourage you to give it a try and set up an account. If you like, take a look at my page if you haven't already. You can see who I follow and who follows me and decide who you would like to see more from. You will find a lot of interesting ideas exchanged; you can participate in the discussion or opt to just watch for a while.

Now, having said that, I also want to encourage you to manage your time wisely when using Twitter or ANY form of social media! It is very easy to log on to social media and spend more time that you had planned before you know it. A quick check of Twitter can easily turn into an hour with all the interesting people, ideas, and articles that present themselves. Set boundaries with yourself and follow them. The last thing you want to do is lose productivity in an area where you were meant to increase productivity!

Another recommendation is to maintain a high degree of professionalism when using social media, whether it is a professional or personal account. Anything you post on the internet can be found with minimal effort and lasts for longer than you ever expected. Keep that concept in mind when writing anything on any social media outlet. "Would I want my clients or referral sources to read this?", is a good question to ask when writing anything anywhere on the internet.

That idea, the "privacy," or lack thereof, of the internet leads to the final social media outlet of the Big Three: Facebook. The settings of Facebook appear to be constantly changing and have been the subject of much frustration just in the short time I have been writing this book. The website has been suspect in its collection and sharing of its users information. For me, that brings concern as to how to use it professionally. I have had a personal Facebook account for a few years, and it has been a wonderful tool to connect with peers and friends. I have my concerns about using it professionally, especially as it relates to our work. Therefore, I've tried to keep pretty firm professional boundaries between my personal account and the professional account of A New Direction Counseling. However, I do recognize that they are connected.

The bottom line for me with Facebook is that I use it sparingly for my professional work. As I already had a personal account, it was an easy decision to utilize some of it's capabilities for my professional work. However, due to the ever-changing security and privacy settings, I use the professional account only to post new article updates and not to connect the "fans" or "followers" of that page as some businesses do.

If you chose to use Facebook as a professional social media tool, familiarize yourself with it's capabilities and flaws, and work within the boundaries of your professional ethics. Through the course of writing this book, Facebook has expanded the capabilities of its "fan pages." This might be the next great evolution for the website, but one that should be well researched in our profession – a profession that values confidentiality and privacy.

Social media is a great tool for building connections. However, we are still just beginning to understand it's true capabilities. I encourage you to give it a try but to be cautious and conscientious of your professional duties to confidentiality and client privacy when using it.

Collaborating with doctors on clients you share

This is the quickest, easiest, most sure-fire, most obvious relationship building concept that will build your practice and community credibility the quickest. Unfortunately, **NOT ENOUGH OF US ARE DOING IT!**

I can even admit that I don't do this enough.

But when I do, it sure helps. Not only does it improve my ability to help my client, it helps their all-round care. Their physician knows what I am thinking, I know what the psychiatrist is thinking, and we are all able to proceed with just a little bit more knowledge of our client and in a unified direction. What a great benefit for the client!

It also benefits our practice. When we do the right thing and coordinate care for our clients, the other attending professionals appreciate and respect us for it. They don't always have the time to chat the very instant we call them, but if you say it is regarding a client/patient that we are mutually helping, you can bet they will be getting back to you at the next possible moment.

In simply calling the physician or psychiatrist you share a client with expresses your professionalism. Sharing your treatment plan and listening to the doctor's goals for the patient share your therapeutic genius with one of the prime referral sources in your community. This is one more way to build your credibility and to inform people, important people in your referral pipeline, about what you do, who you are, and how you can help the community.

Let's talk about that client/patient "pipeline," a term I use to describe how many individuals find their way to counseling when they don't even initially realize they need it.

Doctor's offices see dozens (hundreds?) of patients each week. Many of whom are presenting with the issues YOU TREAT – but the patient doesn't always know, they just know that they aren't feeling "right" – they may be depressed, anxious, stressed, struggling with ADHD etc. But they don't know to find YOU.

They do know to go their doctor, though.

If their doctor knows the symptoms and is able to realize that it is anxiety, depression, ADHD, or stress, AND the doctor knows that you work with people struggling with these issues – well, it's a natural decision for the doctor to help the patient move on the counseling – to move on to the professional who is going to be able to continue to help. It just makes sense, right?

Unfortunately there are a few obstacles there – obstacles that YOU can influence and remove for potential clients and referral sources. Removing obstacles makes you a hero and a valued member of the community. So let's go remove some obstacles.

The first obstacle may be the doctor's ability to recognize the symptoms of ADHD, stress, depression, anxiety, bipolar disorder, etc. Most of them do, but some don't. It's our job to make sure they know. It's our job to make sure that they know the best treatment for patients is a COMBINATION of medication (physician/psychiatrist specialty) AND talk therapy (our specialty). You can do this in a variety of ways. You can send them research you've found, write up summaries for them, and share the information that supports the cooperation of medical and therapeutic work. Once you establish that relationship, meet with them to share about the latest innovations in our combined fields. Doctors are SUCH busy people these days, I have found that they greatly appreciate any opportunity to quickly and easily consume new information. We can be their source for great information that helps them, our clients, and our communities.

The next stumbling block for physicians is knowing what you do once they recognize the symptoms. They need to know that you are in the community to support them and help their patients – your clients.

That is where working with the physicians and psychiatrists of your clients comes in. As I mentioned previously, beating down doctors doors to show them your bright shining smile and newly printed brochure is not as effective as building a relationship with them that is based on helping your community and shared clients. You build respect and appreciation in working with them in a collaborative fashion.

On the other hand, you are just another drug company rep, surgical device salesman, or vendor when you come knocking on their door handing out your business card. I've been there, I was that guy…

The goal is to build mutually helpful relationships with those doctors. Get out there and show them how you are helping your clients – their patients. One goal you can set is to take an hour each week to make those calls.

"Only one hour?!" Yes, only an hour.

Let's face it, they are not always (never) going to be available exactly at the time you call. Be prepared for that. Leave your name, number, maybe even your cell number, and the reason for your call (I am taking for granted that you already secured a release from your client – PLEASE make sure you do this!). When the physician returns your call, and they almost always do when it comes to discussing patients, have that conversation about the client and share your genius. Let them know who you are and what you do by simply talking about the amazing work you are doing with the client and how it is helping the client and the doc.

There are opportunities to build relationship at every turn. Building working relationships with doctors, networking with other professionals in your community, getting your message out into the world through writing and public speaking; these are all great opportunities to build your practice in a successful and personally authentic manner. You don't have to engage in slick sales tactics or *"icky-feeling"* marketing talk. You can speak about who you are and what you do – authentically, professionally, and in a way that feels right to you. In doing that, you will attract the right referral sources and the right clients for who you are and how you work.

In the end, I think it all starts with **knowing who you are, at what you do**. That may be the hang-up for a lot of us who struggle in practice. At times, there seems to be too much information that confuses us into adopting a message that may not be authentically ours. It takes some work for us to figure this out. But when you do, you will find your practice message flows easily from it.

Take some time to understand this. It may be a good time to take a break and ask yourself that question, "Do I know who I am as a helping professional?" If you feel you haven't quite figured out who you are and what you do in a personal and/or professional sense, now might be the time to think about investing in your own personal growth – either through your own therapeutic work or coaching.

It's a fairly well-known fact that therapists, counselors, social workers, and psychologists should engage in their own therapeutic work to be the best that they can be. It's an equally well know fact that **only a small percentage** of us actually go about that process. Maybe now is your time – if you are struggling with moving forward or defining who you are I encourage you to think about it. Supervision and therapy are great for personal and professional growth, as is coaching. They have their different focuses and purposes, I have found that participating in all of them at various stages of my life and career have produced considerable benefit. It has helped me to be who I am today.

Know who you are, know what you do, and know how to share that message with your community.

5

Your Website as Your Primary Marketing Strategy

Your website is the single most critical, useful, and necessary component of your practice.

This is a platform from which all kinds of amazing and enterprising therapeutic endeavors can be launched. It is the starting point and ending point for promoting the work you do.

It is the first thing most people will see about you. It is where they will formulate their first impression about you. It is a living, breathing business card. It is an ever-changing and always-evolving representation of your practice and the work you do.

An effectively crafted website combines all the best components of sales, marketing, and relationship building in an authentic manner.

It is simply the best thing you can do for your business.

And, probably, the single most significant factor for success.

Have I hyperbolized enough to convince you?

Why is a website so critical?

It is your living, breathing business card.

Your business card used to be all you had for potential clients or referral sources to remember you by. You would meet someone, hand them your business card after the exchange, and hope that they remembered you, what you did, and where they placed your card when the time they needed your services came.

Today, your website is a changeable, adaptable business card. It is an opportunity to continuously and strategically reconnect with your potential client or referral source. It also offers them a chance to find out more about you, more than just name, address, and phone number. You can update your website as often as you like; daily, weekly, monthly, or never. If you want to add something – a new service, or a product, and you want people to know about it, it can be up one your website quickly and inexpensively.

A website, done right, soothes potential clients who may be nervous about starting therapy – it gives them insight into your philosophy, style, and personality. People want to know MORE about you before they enter into a therapeutic relationship with you – this is your opportunity to build trust and share who you are and what you do in an authentic and personal manner. When done right, your website gives potential referral sources additional information to pass on to their client or patients so that they feel comfortable making a referral. If they don't have a stack of your business cards in their office, they can refer potential clients to your website so that they can get in touch with you.

This is where people find businesses today.

Research continues to point to the fact that more and more people are using the internet to locate health service providers. A 2009 Gallup survey indicates nearly half of all Americans are "frequent" internet users – meaning they use the internet for an hour or more EACH DAY. You can read the exact demographic breakdown at http://www.gallup.com/poll/113638/nearly-half-americans-frequent-internet-users.aspx .

The study offers a thought provoking summary:

Americans are using the Internet more frequently than ever. While the most educated, most affluent, and youngest Americans are those more likely to say they use the Internet more than one hour per day, the less affluent, non-working, and unmarried are increasing their usage at noteworthy rates. Overall, the shifts recorded over the past year suggest that some of the historical gaps in Internet use across demographic groups may be narrowing. If these changes continue, it would represent an important closing of the economic and educational Internet divides.

With the Internet still in its infancy according to most technology experts, it is reasonable to anticipate continued growth in use among all of these sectors in the years to come. At the same time, the fact that several groups show either stable or declining usage certainly gives rise to the question of whether some sort of plateau is possible. In either case, business leaders -- and advertisers in particular -- will be well-served to keep these burgeoning trends in mind. While targeting content toward the most educated, most affluent, and youngest Americans may be an effective strategy today, the growth evident among their counterparts at the other end of the spectrum suggests new strategies may be needed to cater to the frequent Internet users of tomorrow.

What does this mean for you and I?

This information can impact us in a variety of ways. The single most important factor when it comes to marketing your practice is this: no matter who your ideal client is; who it is you work best with, more and more they will be looking for you online or on their smartphone. If you do not have a web presence, you will be missing out on a chance to serve them.

Have I sold you on the idea yet?

If you are ready to get started on your website, or if you are wondering where to start, there are a variety of ways to go about it.
I've used several methods, and I am sure for each one I have employed, there are a dozen more.

For my first counseling site, I learned how to use Homestead.com. It's a very basic point-and-click system that allows you to make your own website for around $10-20 per month. It's not the prettiest looking group of sites, but it gets the job done on a budget. I like the fact that I controlled the site from start to finish and was able to make updates whenever I wanted without having the hassle or cost of having a "web person" take care of it. I think the do-it-yourself mentally of using homestead helped me to really take ownership of the site and what I wrote on it. The down side, of course, was that it was time consuming.

My next incarnation of my site was created by a web development company, one owned and operated locally by a business acquaintance. The positives were that because they were a web company, the site could be done quickly and it looked much better than what I could do.

Of course, the down side was cost, this time in the form of dollars instead of time. With handing over control of the site to another entity, I had to wait (time cost) and pay (money cost) for each update or addition I had to the site. I didn't like that very much.

> "Your website is an extension of you and your work. It will be the first impression people get of you, and critical in their decision making process to choose to work with you."

Because of that, I am in the process of a third website redesign as this book is being written. I have hired a professional to use the WordPress system to create the site. Once it is up and running, I will take charge of updates and additions, once I finish reading WordPress for Dummies.

You can choose to have as much or as little control of your website as you want. Learn coding, or a system of website design like WordPress, and create your own; or you can farm it out to a web development company.

You have a lot of choices. The one choice I don't think you have is NOT having a site.

How can I use my website to the fullest?

Write from your voice, not your Master's thesis or a greeting card.

This is likely to be the most difficult, but most essential, parts of creating your website. Your website is an extension of you and your work. It will be the first impression people get of you, and critical in their decision making process to choose to work with you. In order to be truly authentic and to insure the "right" clients choose to work with you, you must learn to write from your own voice.

This can be difficult when we consider how important our website is in generating new business. However, I want to encourage you to think of it more as your website being critical in generating "the right kind of business" for you. When you write your website copy in your voice, you can't help but connect with people who want to work with you. This is "the right kind of business." But when you try "too hard" or when you write from "someone else's voice" it comes out wrong, you attract the wrong kind of client for your work, and it will leave you feeling inauthentic.

I know I have a tendency to want to severally "over-professionalize" everything I write – from my website, to my articles, to my correspondence – it just doesn't work in those situations.

Save your tendency to write overly-professional, jargon-filled prose for court reports and insurance documentation. When it comes to writing to and for your clients or potential clients, you have to write to them in YOUR voice. This is your opportunity to let them get to know you, and your style of working with people, therefore, your writing should be a natural extension of that work.

Of course, there is the other extreme as well. If we are not writing from our jargon-filled "scientist-practitioner" state of mind, we may have a tendency to write from the overly flowery, "save the world" voice. I know I have. In my efforts to steer clear of a tendency to write in the form of a grad school textbook, I adopted the overly emotional, how-can-I-save-you style. That doesn't work either. Not only does it feel personally inauthentic, but I'm fairly certain it annoys and alienates potential clients with its condescending verbiage.

It's tough to find the middle ground. The best way I can tell you to do it is to write in YOUR own voice. Write in the way you would speak to a client. Obviously, the more you practice, the more you write, the easier it will become to recognize your voice.

One way to conceptualize this is to think about how you can help your clients, and write about that. Some advocate to "think about what keeps your potential clients awake at 3 A.M." then write about how you can help them with that concern or issue.

Tell your clients how you are going to help them, not what your specialties are. I don't recommend listing the methods, techniques, and theories you prefer to work within when helping, but share the parts of your work that are going to help your clients.

> Instead of "I use a cognitive behavioral model…"
>
> Try, "*we will work on developing different ways of thinking and interacting with the world…*"
>
> Or "*…develop a repertoire of skills and ideas to help you work through your concerns…*"
>
> Rather than "*EMDR to treat posttraumatic stress disorder…*"
>
> What about "well-researched and effective techniques to help you overcome past experiences…"
>
> "Family systems theory to re-establish parent-child attachment"
>
> Is not as welcoming as "*looking at how communication and interaction between family members can improve…*"

The idea is to replace cold and impersonal jargon with warm action word; the words that operationalize what we really do, rather than the words we were given in grad school.

It takes time and effort to find your voice. It has taken me quite a while. I have been through two websites, and I am currently working on a third redo, mostly to "change my voice." What has helped me has been the process of trial and error. Failure and getting up to do it again.

What has REALLY helped has been writing weekly articles, and then hearing the feedback of friends, peers, and my wife. My close friends and loved ones serve as a great barometer for my writing –they know me well enough to know my voice, and they feel comfortable enough to offer constructive criticism. It's not always nice to hear, but it has certainly helped me grow. If you are going to write updateable material, good content, and I highly encourage you to do so, I encourage you to enlist the feedback of several close professional peers and personal friends. Ask them to serve as your own personal writing barometers to offer insight in to when you are speaking in your voice and when you are writing from a textbook.

The other great way to discover your own voice is to read a lot of other works. I try to read as much diverse material as possible in order to expand my own ability to write. It's amazing how the styles of Jimmy Buffett, William Gibson, Bill Bryson, and Rainn Wilson can all be so different but equally as engaging in their diversity. They all write in their own voice, and they all find a way to keep me engaged in their work. That can be the same for you – there are a million different ways to share the same idea in your own voice. Find your voice, and start writing from it. Use your voice to create your website content and then go on to write for your clients on a more regular basis.

Updating information – writing helpful and insightful content for clients and potential clients on a regular basis

I believe this is one of the leading factors, website or otherwise, that sets successful therapists apart from struggling therapists. It takes a considerable amount of discipline, investment, and motivation to start this process. Once you do, once you build it into your professional life, it becomes your new norm. Once that happens, you will be amazed at what this one to two hours per week can do for you and your practice. Once you build this heightened investment, discipline, and motivation into your writing, it will permeate your practice.

The nuts and bolts are simple, and generally consist of a few software applications, with bit of work.

The first part is to have an updateable portion of your website – a blog, article section, "recent writings", etc. I really like the functionality of WordPress; and, as I said, I have also used Homestead.com to build my own sites with blogs. There are plenty of places out there to get started. The important thing is to get started. For me, I like to have the article as the front or home page of my website. The page people go to first when going to my website. There are a few reasons why:

Frequently changing your website front page and giving people a reason to go there improves your site rankings in search engines. I want a reason for people, especially potential clients to visit my site more often. It helps them move from "potential" to "I want to work with this guy – he can help me". Additionally, if I don't like what is on the front page this week, I know it will be changing next week. There is something good about knowing you can change what people see and what they read on your front page, the "impression forming" information, whenever you want.

How to add the power of writing to your website and practice

> *Step 1* - Build your website using WordPress, or Blogger, or Homestead, or any one of the blogging/website services out there. You can take the time to learn any one of these systems yourself, or hire it out for somewhere around $700-1,400. One way will cost time and a little bit of money, the other way will cost money, and a little bit of time. You get to choose.

> *Step 2* – Write content – write GOOD content. Offer something useful to your clients on a weekly basis. There are some therapists who write monthly, and some professionals out there who write daily. For me, and I think for us, weekly seems to be optimally – it allows us time to do our daily work, see clients. But weekly also requires a bit more discipline and creativity than monthly work.

For those struggling with the idea of creating content, it really is VERY EASY. There is SO MUCH out there to write about. I highly recommend you create a way to capture your ideas as they happen. I carry a small notebook on me most of the time, or I jot notes in my smartphone, or I use a document labeled "Writing Ideas" on my laptop. Ideas pop up all the time, I want to make sure I capture them in the moment, before they vanish – and they do. Develop a system of capturing ideas in your daily activities, and you will be amazed at how easy it is to come up with something to write about each week.

The **EASY** part – where I find ideas.

Life – How many times each day do we find a situation related to something one our clients is dealing with, or think a particular client would benefit from knowing? My struggles in parenting, triumphs in marriage, difficulties as a working person, frustrations with society, joys in the world – these have all been topics for writing in the past few years. Each one of these topics started as an event in my life that I noticed, jotted down, and wrote about later on. Certainly you encounter one situation each week that would benefit a current client, or potential clients.

Tools – How many different tools do we use throughout our week as helping professionals? Take ten minutes at the end of your week to think about the different ideas or concepts you shared with a client.

Here are just a few:

The Basics of Communication	MASLOW'S HIERARCHY
IRRATIONAL THINKING	Self-talk
Thought Stopping	PARENTING & DISCIPLINE
BIRTH ORDER	Depression Medication
Dealing with Anxiety	MEDITATION AND DEEP BREATHING
PROCHASKA & DICLEMENTE'S STAGES OF CHANGE	

Those are just what I thought of off the top of my head. I am certain you can come up with far more. That brief list is almost three months of weekly articles ideas just waiting for you to start writing about.

Other media – There's a wealth of knowledge out there and a million ways to find it. I will share the ways I get it, and I am sure for each way I share, you can come up with five more.

Movies - I love to watch movies, but I don't get a chance to very often. So when I do get the opportunity, I am sure to make a selection my family and I will enjoy. Each time I am delighted at the wealth of possibility to write about. Whether it is science fiction or a "chick flick", old or new, adult drama or children's comedy, there is always something to be written about. In particular, when it comes to working with families, I am amazed at the wealth of helpful information contained in the latest wave of animated movies, or, for that matter, the classics too.

> **Reading** – If you read 200 or 300 pages someone else wrote, you are sure to come up with a few words or ideas of your own to share. Authors I have appreciated and shared: Malcolm Gladwell, John Gottman, Bill Bryson, William Gibson, Rainn Wilson and SoulPancake, Seth Godin, Hugh MacLeod, Jimmy Buffett, Robert Frost, David P. Diana, Irvin Yalom, Mitch Albom, Chris Brogan… the list could go on for quite a while. Here are 13 different authors – each one with some brilliant ideas to share with you – take a look at just one chapter, or one article of theirs, and see what it inspires you to write about.

Some of these authors put out a book every few years, some put out an article each day. You could probably find a year's worth of weekly ideas by researching the authors I just listed. You could probably find another year's worth by reviewing your favorite authors. **There are plenty of ideas to inspire us.** If popular culture reading is not your thing, surely you have a wealth of journal articles, Psychology Today, or other professional writing that you can share with potential clients. I have stacks of Psychotherapy Networkers, Journals of Play Therapy, and Psychology Today magazines sitting around my home and office. What do you read that inspires you? Will your current clients and potential clients benefit from knowing about it?

The bottom line is that opportunity to write in your voice and share with your clients is all around you. All it takes is for you to look for it.

> **Step 2.5 – Write CONSISTENTLY.** As you are making this decision, as you think about whether or not this is the way to go for you, factor in the conviction and motivation it takes to do this consistently. Consistency is the key component to making writing the difference maker between successful and struggling therapists.

As you plan for your budding venture as a therapist/writer, determine the logistics of how you are going to write an article week-in and week-out. Make sure you have planned for consistent writing. Where do you put your one to two hours each week for your article? Are you able to be flexible with your writing? Are you going to write a few back-up articles before you start putting them out in to the world? Whatever your plan, make sure you plan to be consistent. You must be consistent in order for this to be successful.

Writing articles will not bring quick and easy success – it will not fill your practice with your first article. It takes time to build. Small steps, short gains – just like therapy. As we work with our clients to consistently engage in the work we encourage them to do, so must we focus on our own ability to be consistent with our writing.

But it DOES bring success eventually. Consistently writing articles and putting them out in the world through your website, email broadcasts, EzineArticles.com, and various other methods will get you noticed, begin to fill your practice, and provide other opportunities that you may not even have thought of. Did I mention you should do it consistently? Week-in, week-out, without fail, no time for illness, consistently.

> **Step 3** – Share your brilliance with the world. You have taken the time to put together a website, you've written an amazing article with awesome content that can help anyone who reads it, now SHARE it.

The first thing I do with my articles is to feed them into a broadcasting system. I like both Constant Contact and 1ShoppingCart.com. Constant Contact is very simple to use, it builds your email template for you but allows you to alter as needed, and you can update your outgoing emails, or "broadcasts," fairly quickly. I started out with a "free sample" and really liked it. For $15 per month, you can use the service as many times as you want to send emails out to up to 500 recipients. 1ShoppingCart offers a little bit more, so it costs a little bit more and is a little more complex to use. I work with a virtual assistant to update and create templates for 1SC, but I do the weekly work of putting in a new article and setting it to go out.

That's the other great thing about these services; no matter when you write your articles, once you put your article in to the template, you can set it to go out at whatever time you want. My Mental Health and Wellness articles from A New Direction Counseling go out at 8:55 A.M. EST every Monday morning, and The Therapist's Sherpa articles go out every Tuesday morning at 9 A.M. EST (except for that one time when I was taking over the weekly duties from my virtual assistant, and I didn't know you were supposed to press the "send" button – see "Failures"). These systems allow me to put in the article and send it at the same time each week whether I wrote it a week before, a month before, or five minutes before it goes out. I can set it to go out while I am sleeping or awake. They are great systems to employ.

No matter when I write the articles, the get emailed out to those who want to receive them at the same time each week. From there, I post them to my websites. I try to do this close to the time when the articles are emailed out, but it doesn't always happen that way. In fact, it rarely does any more. I used to be fairly neurotic about posting to the website RIGHT AFTER the article was emailed out. That got to be too, well, neurotic. I was causing myself excess stress for no reason. Now, I will update the blog the day before, or the day the email goes out; generally within 24 hours before or after the email.

After that, I promote the heck out of my articles to my toughest critics, my friends, peers, current clients, potential clients, and referral sources, using Twitter, Facebook, and LinkedIn. I'll share a link to it on Twitter a few times a day for the week it is new, so that the helping professionals and social media people I "follow" and who "follow" me can have a read. This is also an opportunity to connect with other professionals; that's why I may put out a link to the article at 1 P.M. AND 1 A.M. You would be amazed who is out there reading psychology articles at one o'clock in the morning! I share with friends and family via Facebook, and "fans" of A New Direction Counseling as well. Finally, anything that is Tweeted through Twitter is automatically posted to my LinkedIn account.

Not one of these social media outlets has ever yielded a client directly. That is, never have one of my friends (Facebook), followers (Twitter), or professional associates (LinkedIn) ever become a client. However, some clients become fans of A New Direction Counseling on Facebook, or they will follow @Think_Change on Twitter. There have been times that the "top-of-mind awareness" caused by these social media opportunities has helped a friend or follower think of me when they knew someone in their social circle who needed counseling.

I bring this to your attention for two reasons. First, if you are going to use social media, you have to be very aware of your boundaries using it. My LinkedIn account is totally business, as is my Twitter account.

Do I post more than just articles?

Absolutely. It is "social" after all.

But I work very hard to keep even my most amusing of thoughts as professional as possible. When it comes to Facebook, I use it more for social connections with old friends, but I also realize that there is the potential for professional connections to find out about me or my business on Facebook, therefore I may be a little bit more social but still professional.

It is important to be mindful of what you are putting on the internet, regardless of the device you use to put it out there. Whatever you write to the internet can be found, regardless of the "security" you use. Therefore, I encourage you to be authentically professional in everything you do – have fun – but be mindful of the image you are creating for yourself.

Finally, I will share my articles through EzineArticles.com, or Ehow.com, About.com, or Ask.com – I am sure there are plenty more "dot-coms" where you can share. I know a lot of my peers will share through blogs on Psychology Today.com or PsychCentral.com. The bottom line is share. Share where ever you feel your audience can find you. You have a great wealth of knowledge in your area and unique experience in your life. The world will benefit from hearing about it. Share.

There it is, the *simple 3.5 step process* to building credibility, expert status, and your practice; ALL IN UNDER two HOURS A WEEK! I don't think it gets any easier than that:

Step 1 - Build it – Use a website or blog that is updateable using WordPress, Blogger, Google, Yahoo Blogs, Homestead.com or any other one of the available website engines out there; or have someone build it for you.

Step 2 – Write it - Find your inspiration and motivation and write a bunch of articles – have some back-up articles or write for a month at a time if you are worried about being able to do it all.

Step 2.5 – Do it CONSISTENTLY – Each week, without fail (or each day, or each month but recommend weekly.)

Step 3 – Share it – You are already an expert in your field, in your area of expertise – the world deserves to know about your brilliance. Find the outlets and avenues that you like to use most, the places your potential clients and referrals sources use most, and share your genius with them.

The "Share It" component to sharing articles deserves some additional time, particularly the idea of building a list of people to whom you email your articles. This is an especially sensitive topic in our time.

First, you must have permission to mail your information to these people – please make sure you secure their permission. This can easily be done with a simple "sign up" box on your website. You can encourage people to go to your site and sign up, or people can sign up on their own because they like what they see. However the process goes, it is important that they sign up. It is important that they give permission for you to email them. You must ask their permission.

The other fact is that it takes time to build this list of people. Please give it time before you begin to think about giving up. I started out with about 25 people – mostly clients who I ASKED PERMISSION to send articles to or whom I encouraged to sign up to receive the articles. There were also a few college friends I asked permission to send to so that they could critique the writing for me. They eventually shared the opportunity with others, as did my clients. From there, it took about six months to get to 100 subscribers, and then it blossomed from there.

Give it time. Even the internet marketing gurus and moguls took some time to build up their lists of interested people, and they are in the business of being internet marketing gurus and moguls! You are in the business of being a therapist, typically meaning 20 to 30 clients per week. You don't need a list of 10,000 subscribers any time soon, so don't let defeat creep in to your mind or your consistency when it takes time to build your following. It will come.

Using your website as an extension of your business card also provides several other unique opportunities for potential clients and referral sources to get to know you. Video and audio recordings are easier and cheaper to create and post to a website than they ever have been.

You no longer require a studio recording system or full film crew to produce audio or video for your site. I have used small handheld audio recorders and different phone conference and recording systems to record audio interviews and discussion on a variety of topics. Video cameras, especially flip-cams, are quite inexpensive and easy to film, download, and post to your site as well.

Ideas to reach out to your community:

> A video of your office and lobby to help potential client feel at ease
>
> An example or re-enactment of the kind of work you do – different kinds of modalities may work better than some others for this.
>
> An audio or video interview with another community expert, such as a chiropractor, dietician, physician, or pediatrician – somebody related to your specialization
>
> Meditation scripts or music for clients to download and listen to
>
> Monologues on helpful tips, techniques, and coping skill to use at home

I'm sure there are many more possibilities only limited by your creativity. Use your creativity to put yourself in the position of your ideal potential client – what do they want to know about you or see on your website? Invest a small amount in a flip-cam or recorder and put that information on the site. Take the "extension of your business card" idea to its next logical level. This is one more opportunity for you to help potential clients become current clients.

Products
One big way to maximize the use of your website is to offer opportunities to help clients, or potential clients, in other ways through different kinds of helpful informational products. This provides one more avenue for clients to find relief in your work.

This also provides an opportunity for you to earn a little bit more financially outside of individual or family counseling sessions. This is a chance for passive income – a way to help clients and earn a little extra outside of the tradition clinical methods.

Write a book, offer a tip sheet, provide meditational tracks and instructions; there are more ways to offer clients assistance via your website than I can list here – really this idea is an entire book in itself, as the ideas and information is so vast. It's something for you to be thinking about, though, as you plan and design your website.

What is your message?
When you look at your marketing process, the entire process begins and ends

with this idea, "What is your message?" For the sake of this book, we are ending with this concept. It is a bit more philosophical than it is "nuts and bolts," but requires just as much, if not more, of your attention, as it is the basecamp from which you launch your entire private practice journey.

There are quite a few theories and ideas on how to formulate your message for the public. I think all of them are right in different ways. This is such a deeply personal and philosophical question, that it really is unique for each of us as helping professionals.

Answering this question requires time to think and a desire to ponder how and why we want to help people. It doesn't get more personally philosophical than that. I cannot answer the question for you, but I can give you some tips on how to arrive at your answer.

Give yourself time, and I don't mean just one day focused on answering the question, but let it evolve over time. You may find your answer to the question and craft your message today, only to find that it changes next year. I think that's OK. **We change as people. Our practice is a reflection of us. Therefore, our practice and our message will change.** The important part is that we take the time to purposefully and authentically focus on what that message is. Just as businesses and corporations have weekly, monthly, and yearly strategy meetings, so should we. This is the time to consider our ever-changing message and the heart of our practice.

Let the message evolve. As my practice has evolved, my message has evolved. At one time, I was afraid of letting that happen. I thought I had to "stand firm". That only brought personal dissatisfaction and professional inauthenticity. By allowing myself, my practice, and my message to evolve, I recognized it was OK to change and grow – just like we help our clients to see.

Craft a short-form and long-form message. The short-form is what many marketing gurus and experts call "The Elevator Speech," the message that you can rattle off in 30 seconds or less to inform someone about what you do. I used to be a huge fan of The Elevator Speech but not so much anymore. There is just so much to what we do as practitioners of mental health and helping sciences, that it may not be possible to sum up everything in less than 30 seconds. It's almost a direct contradiction to the idea of having a website as a "living, breathing, business card." If we are going to do that, then how can we boil it all down into 30 seconds?

The simple answer is that we can't.

However, we must.

So I encourage you to think of what your 30-to-60 second message would be. Do you simply say "I am a therapist"? Or do you think of something more creative to share, like "I help families rebuild communication and connection through a variety of play-based interactions," or "I help people struggling with alcohol and substance abuse reclaim their lives." It's your message describing what you do and who you are, use your therapeutic creativity to make it a solid and substantial message.

From there, you can take the time to craft the long form, the meat and potatoes, the brilliant insight that you will build your website, brochures, advertising, and relationship-building material from.

Once you do, share it. I'd love to read it. I am sure our peers would as well. I think we are all in the process of continually crafting our message and allowing ourselves and our practices to evolve.

The more we share what we are working on, and how we are working on it, the better we will all get at it.

6

You are Your Business- The Personal Side of Private Practice

It may seem odd to include a "personal" section in a book on the business of building a private practice business.

I rationalize that with this idea, as helping professionals, we are not producing and selling widgets; we are not mining raw material to produce a product. *In private practice WE ARE OUR BUSINESS*. You are your business. The core of your business, helping others, relies mightily on who you are. It relies entirely on who you are.

You are the machine that makes your business go.

When that machine is working well, when all the components are working in unison, the product is one of the most amazing available.

When that machine, or any one of its components, is in the least bit deficient or worn, the entire machine can seize up.

Don't let that happen to your business. Don't let that happen to your machine. Don't let it happen to you.

Lack of personal care has been the downfall of too many therapists and too

many private practices.

How to do it
How to "prevent burnout"
The first step, you have already taken – entering into, or considering entering into private practice, becoming the commander of your own ship, the Sherpa of your own journey, the guide of your own destiny.

Recognize that and embrace it. Treat yourself appropriately.

I think that comes first in recognizing the difference in what we do; the differences in "helping versus working". We are helpers by nature, but our work is also helping. That may tend to blur the lines sometimes.

The way I see it blurring the lines is by living the message we were taught in grad school, "You are never going to make any money doing this." That message, all alone, devalues the work we do. It tells us that because we are "helpers" we are not "workers" or "business-people," therefore we do not deserve to "earn."

I have witnessed too many private practices fail because the therapist could not get comfortable with their own value as a helping professional, as a business person. They were not able to get comfortable with believing they deserved a fair amount of money for their services. This has been the struggle of many good therapists.

Let me ask you, how can you teach others to value themselves, if you do not value yourself and the work you do?

You DESERVE a fair income for your work, and your clients DESERVE to invest in the work you are doing with them.

If you do not ask for and receive a fair income for your services, resentment and its friend bitterness are not far behind. It is not healthy for you, or for your clients, for you to be working with them from a position of resentment.

If you do not ask for a fair rate, you are not valuing your own work, and neither will your clients. They will be less invested financially and less invested mentally and emotionally. They will do the work hard in and out of session with you. You will soon be working harder than they are.

If you don't become comfortable with charging and received a fair rate, your bills will pile up, and you will be just as stressed, if not more stressed, than you were in previous jobs. You cannot be effective with your clients in helping them de-stress and conquer their anxieties if you are operating from a position of anxiety.

Finally, and most bluntly, if you do not receive a fair rate, you just won't be in business long. Rent, electric, phone, internet, and marketing all have monthly and yearly costs you need to pay. You have to earn on top of these expenses in order to take anything home – that requires being comfortable with, asking for, and receiving a fair rate for your services.

If you feel you ARE asking for a fair rate, EXCELLENT! Good for you! But if you believe you are asking for a fair rate but you are stressed out about finances, you may need to question yourself on that. Are you really asking for fair payment, do you have enough clients?

If your math is correct, "fair rate" multiplied by "enough clients" equals abundance. Anything short of that should be cause to check your math, or your variables.

So if you are struggling with money, bills, or finances in general, you may need to do some personal work on the concept of **Abundance**.

Let's address the shadow of Abundance – Excess. When I talk of therapists living in Abundance, I do not mean excess – not "too much," but "just enough." Abundance is just enough money to have the things we would like to have in life to be comfortable, happy, and satisfied, without lapsing over into having too much that it brings stress back into our lives with a vengeance.

Abundance is having just enough free time away from work that we can cultivate and grow our relationships with friends, loved ones, and peers. Enough time to engage in meaningful hobbies and play in order to model it for our clients. Abundance is not having so much time that we become bored or self-destructive with the excess time we have.

Abundance is a state of mind where we know we have the resources to be "OK," but that it's not "too much," too excessive that we are under more stress because of our excess resources. It is a state of mind and belief that helps us to be at peace and serene, so that we can be fully present with our clients and model the behaviors and attitudes that will help them to find what they need in life.

For me, it is a concept I need to work on frequently, as I still have some of those demons of "you're not good enough," or "you will never make any money," or "noble poor" that creep up to stress me out every now and then. These are concepts that are not healthy for me, and not of benefit to my clients. Abundance, and my being comfortable with seeking it and living it, puts those demons to rest, and allows me to be fully present and engaged with those I work with.

If you are not comfortable with Abundance, you must ask yourself "why?" What do you need to do to become comfortable with it? This is a deeply personal question that I encourage all therapists in private practice to consider. How do you become comfortable living in abundance? What does it mean to you? How do you actively seek it, achieve it, and share it with those you work with? How does you living in abundance enrich the lives of those clients your work with?

To be successful in private practice, and I'm talking just the very basic definition of success, a practice that is viable over the years, you have to become comfortable with the concept of Abundance. It takes work. I look forward to hearing you how you do at it.

I'll share a little bit about how I do it, how I try to stay comfortable with Abundance and live with it so that I can share it with my clients.

Hobbies

If you've been working for an agency for too long, you may have found that you have lost your ability to engage in fun and invigorating activities outside of work.

This is not good.

Not only does it rob you of your own life, but it makes you a boring person who has little to share with your clients other than psychoanalytic or cognitive behavioral theory.

Sadly, I have talked to too many therapists who have allowed this to happen. They have allowed their work to crowd out their life, and they have lost the capacity for hobby.

By taking the time to cultivate hobbies and leisure activity, you open yourself up to experience new things in life. Isn't this one of the things we are trying to help our clients to see? Unfortunately, we may have a tendency to avoid that very recommendation, or we have allowed ourselves to avoid it through working too long, too hard and too much.

I have also found that by engaging in a variety of hobbies and leisure I have more to write about and share for my clients. Whether it is a new book I am reading, a hike I am planning or have taken, or a geocaching adventure I have experienced with my family, leisure activity is ripe with life lessons and opportunities to write and connect with your audience.

Most importantly, it is good for you. It helps you to be a happier, healthier person. That helps you to be a better therapist. Being a better therapist means it is easier to attract and maintain clients. Being a better therapist means you help people more effectively.

In the end, hobbies are necessary to run a good business.

Vacation
Ah, the ultimate hobby – vacationing – another important aspect of being a happy, healthy, and effective therapist.

Gone are the days when you only get two weeks to yourself each year, and you have to work five years to earn a third week. Gone are the years when you REALLY want to take your vacation during the third week of June, but so does everybody else so you don't get to. Gone are the times when you have planned your vacation, you have done everything you need to be ready to go, only to be told, "we need you to stick around this week."

In private practice it is up to you when to take vacation. I encourage you to take it as much as possible. I try to take a few days each month and at least a week every few months. We deal with some very difficult and dangerous material day-in and day-out. No, we are not handling toxic waste, nor are we under fire in a desert somewhere, but the emotional work we put in every day can be hazardous to our health if we don't take time away to de-stress, recuperate, and re-energize.

You don't have to take an extravagant trip to the islands each month. Although, if you can swing that, I highly recommend it! A vacation can be as simple as spending a few days at home engaging in hobbies. On the other hand, I do recommend you get away a few times a year – whether to the islands, or just the next town over. There is something about getting away from home and leaving everything, both clinical work and housework, behind. It is the ultimate re-energizing and re-invigorating reset button.

Again, much like hobby, vacation is critical in maintaining our own mental and emotional well-being. We may have become used to not taking time to ourselves throughout the week, or throughout the year. But now, as owner of your own business, it is important to take this time. It is important to your health, and it is important to the health of your business.

> "There is something about getting away from home and leaving everything, both clinical work and housework, behind. It is the ultimate re-energizing and re-invigorating reset button."

Diet and Exercise

The core of self-care; a healthy diet and moderate weekly exercise. I've shared with you my story of how avoiding these two important self-care concepts affected my life. There are millions of stories out there about how engaging in these two critical lifestyle components positively affects people's lives.

If "not enough time" was once an excuse for not taking care of yourself, now that you are in private practice, YOU are in charge of making the time. You must do so.

You are an important part of your immediate community and an important part of our larger community of helping professionals. We need you to be around for as long as you want to work. Take care of yourself so that we can keep you around.

If you haven't been eating well, it is time to start.

If you haven't been exercising, now is the time to start.

You will be amazed at how quickly and easily you start to feel brighter, smarter, and more able to do the difficult emotional work we do every day.
If you don't know where to start, there are resources available to you. You know where to find them. It starts by grabbing an apple instead of French fries. It starts with going for a walk instead of watching TV. From there, the possibilities are endless.

Financial House Keeping
Finally, the last piece of personal advice I have for you about building a private practice may just be the most important.

If you have been accustomed to getting paid the same amount of money every two weeks during your professional career, **that is about to change in the most terrifying and exhilarating manner.** If you have already been in practice for a while, you know all about this; the scary joy that is your weekly trip to the P.O. box (if you are waiting on insurance money) or the financial ups and downs of full client weeks, and light client weeks.

Personally, I love the ability to earn as much as I would like, based on how hard I want to work in a given week. And I enjoy the gamble that is working with insurance companies. I am pretty sure it took some getting used to early on.

There are several strategies that helped:
First, I avoided credit cards of all kinds: major, minor, big chain, small store, business, and personal. Everyone has a credit card to offer, for a price. Before I went in to practice, I made sure all cards were zeroed out and destroyed. Today, I operate on a cash basis for both my business and personal affairs, and that is what I recommend for the therapists I work with starting out. Building a business is stressful enough; you don't need the added stress of credit. Adding that stress, or compounding that stress, can lead to poor business decisions and a quick exit out of private practice.

When starting up, I had a few months worth of bills (two to three) saved up, and I still try to keep it there today at all times. "Try" meaning that it is not always like that, but I try. That way, if things come up – needed office purchases, website updates, conferences, etc., I get to be my own credit card and pay myself back with interest, rather than paying someone else interest to use their money for the month.

Rumor has it that this is a pretty healthy way to live overall, but it is a very important one if you are in private practice.
Building a savings is really the pinnacle of living in Abundance. You get the satisfaction of building something, but the equal satisfaction of not having to go out asking for money when it comes time to make a business or personal purchase.

You are entering into the professional world of a variable reward schedule, to put it in psychological terms. We all know variable rewards are best for building positive behaviors. So in a way, it's good for us. It can be fun, but equally scary at times. The best way to mitigate the "scary" effects is to have savings in place and to avoid having to pay someone else for the use of their money every month.

Maintaining the financial health of your personal affairs and of your business is critical to building a successful and authentic practice. When our affairs are in order and are when we are not strained to pay creditors and unnecessary bills, it is far easier to be giving and abundant with our time. We are also able to be more healthy and stress-free, again passing it on to our clients, who share with other potential clients.

You have a lot to offer. We want you in private practice. We need you in business for as long as you want to be in business. To make that happen, to make it a reality, manage your personal and business affairs wisely. Maintain your mental, emotional, physical, spiritual, and financial health for your own good and for the good of the clients and community you work with.

There it is.
Everything I know about getting a private practice from thought to reality, from dream to concept to opening day and beyond.

All the nuts and bolts you need to get started and keep going for quite a while. All the basics you need to get the ball rolling and keep it going. This is the start to a successful and authentic private practice.
As I wrap up, I want to share this with you:
The basics to starting a practice don't change much. The questions of "do

I accept insurance or not," "niche practice or generalist," "location, location, location," all those things highlighted in this book, those things don't change much.

What is changing is the nature of private practice.

It used to be that you would put your shingle out, attract clients, and work in an office, face-to-face, one-on-one, or with families for 20 to 30 hours per week. You could do this for years and find a lot of satisfaction and make a great living.

> For good or bad, that is changing.
> Healthcare is changing.
> Technology is changing.

Our world – the world of the helping professional – that is changing too.
We will see some opportunities decrease while others increase.
It will not be as "easy" to work with insurance companies and still make a living.

You can now do more to help more people more effectively with the power of modern technology.

Once you get up and running with your practice, it is something to consider. How do you choose to harness modern technology to extend the reach of your practice?

Private Practice 2.0 is evolving. Will you evolve with it?

For now, good luck in using the tools listed here to build your successful and authentic private practice. I look forward to hearing of your accomplishments!

~Dan
February, 2011

Acknowledgements

Those who motivated me, pushed me, pulled me, and have helped me to get to where I am and know it:

Keith, Hoot, Mark, Ryan, Keian, Mason, the rest of The League and your lovely wives; your friendship, camaraderie, and accountability are something I appreciate and cherish. I wouldn't be who I am without you guys. Thanks. The fact that you are trying to figure out why I listed you in any particular order only shows the competitive fire that you have helped keep lit in me.

My high school "homey," Luke. I have no idea why you majored in English, but now I am glad you did. Editor's Note: (I should note that I actually majored in communications. The real question is why did I spend years in a career writing and editing for newspapers/magazines for very little pay. But either way, you're very welcome.)

Nicole and David Diana; thank you for your inspiration, guidance, and hard work to make this happen.

My counseling and coaching cohort, the people I bounce ideas off of daily: Dr. Peg Snyder, Laura Recio, Elizabeth Doherty Thomas, Dr. Susan Giurleo, Dr. Laura Dessauer, Marco Prospero, Steve Borgman, Linda Esposito, Kathy Morelli, and the rest of the ladies who accepted me as the "Token Dude".

My in-laws, Larry and Nancy Sumpter, thank you for your support and understanding, even though you had no idea what I was up to locked away in the office all this time.

To my parents, Jim and Jane Franz, thank you. You're right; you did something right.

Finally to my wonderful wife, Michelle, thank you. I could write another book on why and what, so just thank you.

And for all those who inspire me and convinced me it was a good idea to do this and didn't even know it: Seth Godin, Dennis Miller, Hugh MacLeod, Chris Brogan, Pat Flynn, Jay Rankin, MJ DeMarco, Johnny B. Truant, Steven Pressfield, William Gibson.

If you need a good kick in the pants, if you need a fire lit under you, if you need just one more reason to get into private practice or to choose to do something with your life, any one of these people can get you started; sampling from all of them might blow your mind and cause you to question your reality.

APPENDIX

FINANCIAL AGREEMENT

STATEMENT OF AGREEMENT

AUTHORIZATION FOR TREATMENT OF A MINOR

INITIAL WELLNESS ASSESSMENT (ADULT)

INITIAL WELLNESS ASSESSMENT (CHILD)

NEW CLIENT AGREEMENT

AUTHORIZATION FOR RELEASE

505 Colonial Ct.
Plymouth, IN 46563
(574) 935-4114

FINANCIAL POLICIES 1/11

FEES:

The fee for service is **$ 90.00** per client hour, **$ 125.00** for initial intake sessions. The client hour is based on a 50 minute session. Appointments are scheduled for the 50 minute period unless previously arranged. Should a session go beyond the 50 minutes, there may be additional charges that are billed in 15 minute increments.

If you believe you may be eligible for a fee reduction per this therapist's agreement with the National Health Service Corps, please consult with the therapist.

Fees are due at the time of service and may be paid for by cash or check. Credit cards are accepted.

INSURANCE:

I am contracted with several EAP providers and Insurance companies to provide mental health counseling services. Your fees will be commensurate with your Insurance policy and the contract with that Insurance provider.

If you choose to utilize insurance I will bill your insurance for reimbursement from the insurance company. Be aware that once insurance is filed the insurance company has a right to review your records. Your insurance company also has the ability to dictate frequency of sessions, total amount of sessions, and time of sessions. The insurance reserves to right to make decisions on payment and treatment as seen fit by the insurance company. If you choose to utilize insurance, it is expected that you will assist the therapist in insuring payment from the insurance company, or accept liability for payment.

Billing, for the purpose of insurance reimbursement, will be provided approximately twice per month unless otherwise arranged.

You are responsible for all fees regardless of the decision of your insurance company - unless otherwise indicated by your insurance company. Any fees that might be paid in error by your insurance company remain your responsibility.

APPOINTMENTS:
Appointments are reserved for you each time you visit. This time is kept for you and will not be filled by another client. Therefore, it is expected that you will notify me at least 24 hours in advance of a cancellation or need to change your time. It is my policy to charge the hourly fee of $ 100.00 for any non-canceled appointment or late canceled appointment, unless there is a valid reason.

RESPONSIBLE PARTY:
I have read and understood the above terms of this agreement and accept full responsibility for all fees incurred for
_____.(Client)

_____NAME/SIGNATURE(Responsible Party)
_____DATE

Daniel A. Franz, MA, LMHC, LCAC

505 Colonial Ct.
Plymouth, IN 46563
(574) 935-4114

Statement of Agreement

A positive therapeutic relationship begins with an agreement between the therapist and the client on certain issues regarding the counseling process.

1. Confidentiality of communications between the therapist and the client will strictly be maintained. Information will be released to outside parties only if specifically authorized in writing by the client. Note: The law places certain limits on confidentiality. Confidentiality will not apply in cases of bodily harm to the client or other persons.

2. By signing this agreement it is understood that all information shared during your treatment is confidential and will not be shared without your express written consent. The exception to this policy is information required by your insurance company and/or financial provider. Any other release of information will be at your signed request. Before you sign a release of information for any other source to obtain your records from me I suggest you discuss it with me.

3. By signing this Policy Statement, you (the patient/client and/or parent of a minor) consent to receive mental health services including, but not limited to examination, treatment, diagnosis, or prevention of a mental condition. Such service will be provided within the scope of the provider's license, certification, and training or the scope of the license, certification, and training of those mental health providers directly supervising the services. (in the case of when the insurance company requires physician supervision.)

4. I understand that it is the policy of this provider, that children **may not be left in the reception area without adult supervision,** and that I will make appropriate arrangements for my child's care when I have a scheduled appointment.

5. Appointments missed, cancelled, or rescheduled with less than 24 hours notice will be charged the regular full fee.

6. A confidential message may be left on the therapist's voice mail at any time. I am available 7 days a week to respond to voicemail and email and usually respond to either within 24 hours. However, if you are in crisis, please dial 911 on your phone to receive the help you need.

Client
Signature_____Date_____

Therapist Signature_____Date_____

505 Colonial Ct.
Plymouth, IN 46563
(574) 935-4114

Authorization for Treatment of a Minor

I _____
authorize and consent to **Daniel A. Franz, MA, LMHC, LCAC / A NEW DIRECTION COUNSELING**
to treat my minor child,
_____, Birth Date: _____
_____

and to provide mental health services including but not limited to examination, treatment, diagnosis, or prevention of a mental/emotional condition. I understand that such services will be provided within the scope of the provider's license, certification, and training.

By signing this agreement it is understood that all information shared during treatment is confidential and will not be shared without your express written consent. The exception to this policy is information required by your insurance company, by law, and/or financial provider.

I understand that as a parent of a minor child I may contact the provider to participate in my child's treatment and/or to review progress.

My initials here will verify that I have discussed the non-custodial parent of my minor child and understand that he/she may be contacted to participate in treatment and/or to provide progress on treatment. _____ *(initials)*

By signing this agreement I certify that I have the legal custody and authority to consent to treatment and agree to assist my child in gaining services, including transportation, and sharing of information relevant to the treatment services.

I understand that it is the policy of this provider, that children **may not be left in the reception area without adult supervision**, and that I agree , for the safety of my child, I will not leave my child until they are in session with the provider, and will return at least 10 minutes prior to the end of my child's session.

_____Signature of Parent of a Minor Child
_____Date
_____Witness
_____Date

Initial Wellness Assessment
(Adult)

Client's Last Name: _____ First Name _____

Date of Birth: ____/____/_____ ☐ Male   ☐ Female

Today's Date: ____/____/_____

---

1. Please indicate the PRIMARY problem that has led you to seek help today.
   ☐ Sad or depressed mood ☐ Relationship/family problems
   ☐ General Stress ☐ Anxiety, worries, or fears
   ☐ Occupational Problems ☐ Physical health problems
   ☐ Grief or loss ☐ Substance use problems
   ☐ Other emotional/psychological problems

2. How much have the problems which have led you to seek help bothered you in the past 30 days

	Not at All	A Little	Somewhat	Quite a bit	Very Much
	☐	☐	☐	☐	☐

3. In the past 30 days, to what extent have the problems which led you to seek help interfered with your:

	Not at All	A Little	Somewhat	Quite a bit	Very Much
a. Family life	☐	☐	☐	☐	☐
b. Social life	☐	☐	☐	☐	☐
c. Work, schoolwork, or housework	☐	☐	☐	☐	☐
d. Health and physical well-being	☐	☐	☐	☐	☐

4. Following are problems or complaints that people sometimes have. For each problem please indicate how much that problem has Bothered or distressed you during the past seven days, including today.

	Not Bothered	A Little Bothered	Moderately Bothered	Quite Bothered	Extremely Bothered
a. Nervousness or shakiness	☐	☐	☐	☐	☐
b. Feeling Lonely	☐	☐	☐	☐	☐
c. Feeling sad or blue	☐	☐	☐	☐	☐
d. Your heart pounding/ racing	☐	☐	☐	☐	☐
e. Feeling hopeless about the future	☐	☐	☐	☐	☐
f. Feeling everything is an effort	☐	☐	☐	☐	☐
g. Spells of terror or panic	☐	☐	☐	☐	☐
h. Feeling so restless you couldn't sit still	☐	☐	☐	☐	☐
i. Feelings of worthlessness	☐	☐	☐	☐	☐
j. Feeling suddenly scared for no reason	☐	☐	☐	☐	☐
k. Feeling no interest in things	☐	☐	☐	☐	☐

5. Please tell us how much you agree with the following three statements:

	Strongly Agree	Agree	Not Sure	Disagree	Strongly disagree
a. I feel good about myself.	☐	☐	☐	☐	☐
b. I can deal with my problems.	☐	☐	☐	☐	☐
c. I am able to maintain control over my life.	☐	☐	☐	☐	☐

6. Are you currently employed? (If yes, proceed to question 7 below. If no, skip to question 11 below.)
   ☐ Yes   ☐ No

7. During the past 30 days, how many days were you unable to work because of your physical or mental health? _____ days

8. During the past 30 days, how many days did you work, but had to cut back on how much you got done due to your physical or mental health? _____ days

9. Are you receiving, have you filed, or are you considering filing for disability benefits or workers' compensation?
   ☐ Yes   ☐ No

10. Are you having any recent problems at work?
    ☐ Yes   ☐ No

11. Are you caring for someone in your family who is ill or disabled?
    ☐ Yes   ☐ No

12. In general, would you say your health is:

   Excellent   Very Good   Good   Fair   Poor
   ☐   ☐   ☐   ☐   ☐

13. In the past 30 days, how much have you been bothered by physical pain?

   Not Bothered   A little Bothered   Moderately Bothered   Quite Bothered   Extremely Bothered
   ☐   ☐   ☐   ☐   ☐

14. Do you now have a serious and/or chronic medical condition such as diabetes, cancer, heart disease, asthma, or rheumatoid arthritis?

   ☐ Yes   ☐ No

15. In the past six months, how many times have you seen a medical doctor or used other medical services?
   Zero   1   2-3   4-5   More than 5
   ☐   ☐   ☐   ☐   ☐

16. Have you had a drink or used drugs in the past 30 days?
   ☐ Yes   ☐ No
   (If yes, proceed to question 17. If no, skip to question 23.)

17. In the past 30 days, have you ever felt you ought to cut down on your drinking or drug use?
   ☐ Yes   ☐ No

18. In the past 30 days, have people annoyed you by criticizing your drinking or drug use?
   ☐ Yes   ☐ No

19. In the past 30 days, have you ever felt bad or guilty about your drinking or drug use?
   ☐ Yes   ☐ No

20. In the past 30 days, have you ever had a drink or used drugs first thing in the morning to steady your nerves or get rid of a hangover?
   ☐ Yes   ☐ No

21. How many days in the past week did you have a beer, glass of wine, mixed drink, or shot of liquor? _____ days

22. On a typical day when you have had a drink, how many glasses,

bottles, cans, and/or shots do you drink?
_____#glasses,bottles,cans,and/or shots

23. Please list all medications, vitamins, or herbal supplements taken within the last six months:

Name	Dosage	Prescribing Physician
Taking currently? Yes/No		
_____	_____	_____
_____	_____	_____
_____	_____	_____
_____	_____	_____
_____	_____	_____
_____	_____	_____

Initial Wellness Assessment
(Child & Adolescent)

Child's Last Name: _____ First Name _____

Date of Birth: ___/___/_____ ☐ Male   ☐ Female

Today's Date: ___/___/_____

---

1. What is your relationship to the child for whom you will be completing this questionnaire?
   - ☐ Mother
   - ☐ Father
   - ☐ Stepmother
   - ☐ Stepfather
   - ☐ Grandmother
   - ☐ Grandfather
   - ☐ Foster parent
   - ☐ Other _____

2. Please indicate your child's PRIMARY problem that has led you to seek help for him or her today.
   - ☐ Sad or depressed mood
   - ☐ Physical health problems
   - ☐ Problems functioning at school
   - ☐ Problems within family
   - ☐ Other behavioral problems
   - ☐ Problems with peers
   - ☐ Anxiety, worries, or fears
   - ☐ Other emotional/psychological problems
   - ☐ Substance use problems

Please provide any additional information you think may be helpful:
_____
_____
_____

3. In the past 30 days, how much have your child's problems that led you to seek help bothered.......

	Not at All	A Little	Somewhat	Quite a bit	Very Much
a. .....your child?	☐	☐	☐	☐	☐
b. .....you?	☐	☐	☐	☐	☐

4. How long has your child had the problem for which you are seeking treatment?
   ☐ Less than   ☐ 1 - 3   ☐ 4 - 6   ☐ 7 - 12   ☐ One or

1 month   months   months   months   more years

5. In general, would you say your child's health is:
   Excellent   Very Good   Good   Fair   Poor
   ☐   ☐   ☐   ☐   ☐

6. Does your child currently have a serious and/or chronic medical condition such as diabetes or asthma?
   ☐ Yes   ☐ NO
   If yes, please print the medical condition (s)
   _____

7. In the past six months, how many times has your child seen a medical doctor or used other medical services?
   Zero   1   2-3   4-5   More than 5
   ☐   ☐   ☐   ☐   ☐

8. In general, how much of a problem do you think your child has with the following?

	No Problem	Some Problems	A Big Problem
a. Getting into trouble.	☐	☐	☐
b. Getting along with his or her mother.	☐	☐	☐
c. Getting along with his or her father.	☐	☐	☐
d. Feeling unhappy or sad.	☐	☐	☐
e. His or her behavior at school (or at work).	☐	☐	☐
f. Having fun.	☐	☐	☐
g. Getting along with adults other than his or her mother and father.	☐	☐	☐
h. Feeling nervous or worried.	☐	☐	☐
i. Getting along with his or her brothers or sisters.	☐	☐	☐
j. Getting along with other kids his or her age.	☐	☐	☐
k. Getting involved in activities like sports or hobbies.	☐	☐	☐
l. His or her schoolwork (or doing his/her job).	☐	☐	☐
m. His or her behavior at home.	☐	☐	☐

9. How much have your child's problems caused …

	Not At all	A Little	Somewhat	Quite a bit	Very Much
a. interruption of personal time?	☐	☐	☐	☐	

b. disruption of family routines? ☐ ☐ ☐ ☐ ☐
c. any family member having to do without things? ☐ ☐ ☐ ☐ ☐
d. any family member to suffer negative mental or physical health? ☐ ☐ ☐ ☐ ☐
e. financial strain for your family? ☐ ☐ ☐ ☐ ☐
f. less attention to be paid to any family member because of attention given to your child? ☐ ☐ ☐ ☐ ☐
h. disruption of your family's social activities? ☐ ☐ ☐ ☐ ☐
i. you to miss work or neglect other duties? ☐ ☐ ☐ ☐ ☐

                                                Yes   No

10. Are you currently employed? ☐ ☐
(If yes, proceed to question 11 below; if no, skip to question 13 below)

11. During the past 30 days, how many days were you unable to work because of your child's problems or your own physical or mental health?
_____ Days

12. During the past 30 days, how many days did you work, but had to cut back on how much you got done because of your child's problems or your own physical or mental health?
_____ Days

13. Please list all medications, vitamins, or herbal supplements taken within the last six months:

Name	Dosage	Prescribing Physician	Taking currently? Yes/No
_____	_____	_____	_____
_____	_____	_____	_____
_____	_____	_____	_____
_____	_____	_____	

Questionnaire completed by:
_____Date_____

NEW CLIENT INFORMATION

TODAY'S DATE: _____

CLIENT:
NAME : _____ DATE OF BIRTH _____

ADDRESS WHERE CLIENT RESIDES:
_____

CITY: _____ ZIP CODE
_____

HOME PHONE:
_____ WORK: _____ CELL: _____

EMAIL: _____

EMPLOYER & POSITION OR SCHOOL & GRADE IF A CHILD
_____

SOCIAL SECURITY NUMBER: _____

YEARS OF EDUCATION: _____

MEDICATIONS: _____

PHYSICIAN: _____

DATE OF MARRIAGE: _____

FIRST MARRIAGE? YES OR NO

INSURED: (or responsible party) (if different than above)

NAME OF INSURED: _____
DATE OF BIRTH _____

ADDRESS OF INSURED:
_____

CITY: _____ STATE: _____ ZIP CODE _____
HOME PHONE: _____ WORK: _____
CELL: _____
E-MAIL: _____
EMPLOYER:
_____

SOCIAL SECURITY NUMBER:
_____

YEARS OF EDUCATION:
_____

MEDICATIONS:
_____

PHYSICIAN:
_____

SPOUSE: (of Client or Insured) (or other parent of a child)
NAME : _____ DATE OF BIRTH _____
ADDRESS :
_____

CITY: _____ ZIP CODE _____
HOME PHONE: _____ WORK: _____ CELL: _____
EMPLOYER:
_____

SOCIAL SECURITY NUMBER:
_____

YEARS OF EDUCATION:
_____

MEDICATIONS:
_____

PHYSICIAN:
_____

DATE OF MARRIAGE: _____ FIRST MARRIAGE? YES OR NO

CHILDREN IN FAMILY:
LIST EACH CHILD IN YOUR FAMILY (FIRST & LAST NAME) DATE OF BIRTH AND IF THEY LIVE WITH YOU (use other side for additional children)

NAME: _____ D.O.B. _____ WITH YOU? _____

NAME: _____ D.O.B. _____ WITH YOU? _____

NAME: _____ D.O.B. _____ WITH YOU? _____

NAME: _____ D.O.B. _____ WITH YOU? _____

HAVE YOU HAD PREVIOUS COUNSELING? _____
WHEN _____ WITH WHO? _____

WHY ARE YOU SEEKING COUNSELING NOW?
_____
_____
_____
_____

REFERRED BY: _____

PLEASE CHECK ANY OF THE FOLLOWING PROBLEMS THE CLIENT IS HAVING:

____crying spells   ____frequent irritability   ____upset stomach
____aggressiveness   ____unreasonable fears   ____difficulty getting up
____hyper activity   ____school problems   ____work problems
____angry outbursts   ____depression   ____anxiety
____loss of appetite   ____excessive eating   ____use of drugs/alcohol
____wanting to die   ____bad dreams   ____loss of loved one

COMPLETE IF CLIENT IS A CHILD

NAME OF PERSON WHO HAS PRIMARY PHYSICAL CUSTODY:
_____

ADDRESS:
_____

CITY: _____ ZIP CODE: _____

HOME PHONE: _____ WORK: _____ CELL: _____

NON-CUSTODIAL PARENT NAME:
_____

ADDRESS :
_____

CITY: _____ ZIP CODE _____

HOME PHONE: _____ WORK: _____ CELL: _____

EMPLOYER:
_____

SOCIAL SECURITY NUMBER:
_____

NOTE: Personal information such as your cell phone number and e-mail address are never shared nor are they used for advertising purposes. These are requested to be used as a secondary means for contacting you should the need occur.

DAF/2-09

A New Direction Counseling
505 Colonial Ct.
Plymouth, IN 46563
(574) 935-4114

Authorization for Release/Disclose Information

I _____
authorize and consent to
    Daniel A. Franz, MA, LMHC, CADAC II / A New Direction Counseling

to <u>provide</u> all specified information (verbally or in writing) to:

_____

and to <u>receive</u> all specified information (verbally or in writing) from:

_____

_____

Regarding myself, _____
                Name   Date of Birth
my minor child, _____
                Name   Date of Birth

I understand that the purpose of this disclosure is to coordinate treatment and/or evaluate services for the above mentioned client.

This consent is subject to written revocation at any time except to the extent that information has already been shared in the interim between

This information has been disclosed to you from records protected by Federal confidentiality rules (42 CFR Part 2). The Federal rules prohibit you from making any further disclosure of this information unless further disclosure is expressly permitted by the written consent of the person to whom it pertains or as otherwise permitted by (42 CFR part 2). A general authorization for the release of medical or other information is not sufficient for this purpose. The Federal rules restrict any use of the information to criminally investigate or prosecute any alcohol or drug abuse patient.

authorization and revocation. Unless another date is specified this release will expire in sixty (60) days. Other specified date for expiration: _____

Specified information to be released: _____
_____
_____
_____
_____
_____
_____

Signed: _____
                                              Client
       Date
Signed: _____   _____
       Client   Date
Signed: _____
       Parent/Guardian of Minor   Date
Signed: _____
       Witness   Date

This information has been disclosed to you from records protected by Federal confidentiality rules (42 CFR Part 2). The Federal rules prohibit you from making any further disclosure of this information unless further disclosure is expressly permitted by the written consent of the person to whom it pertains or as otherwise permitted by (42 CFR part 2). A general authorization for the release of medical or other information is not sufficient for this purpose. The Federal rules restrict any use of the information to criminally investigate or prosecute any alcohol or drug abuse patient.

www.danielafranz.com

Made in the USA
San Bernardino, CA
16 March 2013